Be Refreshed is what we need. It is a drink of cool water to those who are parched and weary. More importantly, it is an opportunity to pause our busy lives and come before the King of Kings. Let Him speak life to you each day.

—SHAUNTI FELDHAHN, social researcher
and best-selling author of *For Women Only*

Growing up, my father put a sticker on every mirror in our home that read, "Happiness is a habit, today is the happiest day of my life, I'm God's greatest miracle." As a little girl, these words gave me confidence to face each day. As a woman, I get my strength from attending daily mass and reading the Bible and daily devotionals. *Be Refreshed* will be added to my daily ritual.

—DINA DWYER-OWENS, Cochair of The Dwyer Group, Inc.;
appeared on *Undercover Boss*

As the founder of Sseko Designs, my work is not just my day job. The Lord is inviting me to be a co-creator of a brighter and more just world. I am so grateful for *Be Refreshed* because it recognizes and validates women who are pursuing their calling in the workplace. I am refreshed and energized by the voices of women I deeply admire for using their gifts, passions, and skills to bring light and restoration in the world for their daily work. For many of us, following Jesus means saying yes to the marketplace, and I am so grateful for resources that help us stay grounded and energized in Jesus' love while we pursue our vocations.

—LIZ BOHANNON, Founder, Sseko Designs;
appeared on *Shark Tank*

Be Refreshed: Devotions for Women in the Workplace is a glimpse into the heart of everyday women who are living full lives and caring for their families, work, and communities while putting God first. These devotions are their moments, stories, and history with God. They show how Scripture has been an anchor and foundation in the midst of juggling what can sometimes be just too much. *Be Refreshed* is a fresh wind in your sails, steering you to connect with God and live the full life you are so beautifully called to!

—LAURA STAFFORD,
Designer for Joanna Gaines at Magnolia

Wow! *Be Refreshed* is such a breath of fresh air, with devotionals that speak directly to the issues experienced by women in the workplace. We are moms, wives, daughters, CEOs, managers, employers, and employees. We experience the challenges represented by each of the roles we occupy on any given day. How refreshing to have a devotional that speaks to *us*, giving us wisdom and perspective as we navigate our days. This is truly life-giving and life-altering. Well done Diane, Jordan, and team!

—ERIN BOTSFORD, CEO of Botsford Financial Group;
Author of *The Big Retirement Risk: Running out of Money before You Run out of Time*; Guest on *Wealth Track* with Consuelo Mack; named multiple times to *Barron's* magazine list of "The Top 100 Independent Financial Advisers" and "The Top 100 Women Financial Advisers"; 4word Board Member

Along with inspirational reflections to spur you on as you head for work, *Be Refreshed* contains an added bonus—the welcome reminder coming from the collective voices in this book that you are not alone. You belong to a growing company of women God is calling to serve Him in the workplace. Be refreshed!

—CAROLYN CUSTIS JAMES, Author of *Half the Church: Recapturing God's Global Vision for Women* and *The Gospel of Ruth: Loving God Enough to Break the Rules*; 4word Advisory Board Member

Be Refreshed: Devotions for Women in the Workplace provides a daily God-centered time to help you through life's challenges, especially as a working woman of faith. I love the practical but very meaningful tips that quickly get to the core of what we all typically struggle through: e.g., anxiety, hectic schedules, leading others, ambition, worries, and balancing work and family. Turning to *Be Refreshed*, with its inspirational Scripture and reflections, has helped ground me in God's loving presence each day.

—MARISSA PETERSON, former COO of Sun Microsystems; former 4word Advisory Board Member

Christian women today are running businesses, leading nonprofits, raising children, volunteering at church, and serving as devoted wives and friends. I have no doubt God is using these women powerfully for his purposes. But all this easily brings with it exhaustion and depletion—which is why this deep yet digestible devotional from Diane Paddison is a key resource for today's professional women. Short daily reflections from a variety of leaders are a great way to start each busy day.

—KATELYN BEATY, *Christianity Today* Editor at Large; Author of *A Woman's Place: A Christian Vision for Your Calling in the Office, the Home, and the World*

Be Refreshed

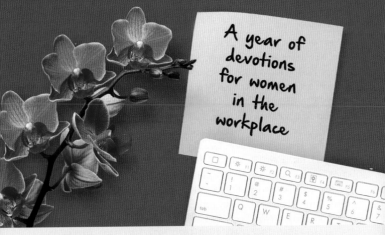

A year of
devotions
for women
in the
workplace

Diane Paddison

WITH JORDAN JOHNSTONE AND
OTHER WOMEN FROM 4WORDWOMEN.ORG

FOREWORD BY Cheryl Bachelder
AND Commissioner Sharron Hudson

BroadStreet
PUBLISHING

BroadStreet Publishing® Group, LLC
Racine, Wisconsin, USA
BroadStreetPublishing.com

Be Refreshed: Devotions for Women in the Workplace

ISBN-13: 978-1-4245-5565-9 (hardcover)
ISBN-13: 978-1-4245-5565-6 (e-book)

Stock or custom editions of BroadStreet Publishing titles may be purchased in bulk for educational, business, ministry, fundraising, or sales promotional use. For information, please e-mail info@broadstreetpublishing.com.

Cover design by Garborg Design
Typesetting by Katherine Lloyd at theDESKonline.com

Printed in China
17 18 19 20 21 5 4 3 2 1

Foreword

By Cheryl Bachelder

My career has given me the opportunity to serve in a variety of leadership roles at companies like Domino's Pizza, The Gillette Company, The Procter & Gamble Company, and most recently at Popeyes® Louisiana Kitchen, Inc. as CEO. At every company, my goal has been to guide those around me to work together and "make beautiful music" as a team. But frankly, there were few role models to help me learn how to do this in a way that was congruent with my beliefs.

As you begin to read this devotional, I applaud you, as a woman in the workplace, for recognizing your need for guidance and encouragement from other leaders like you. In the professional world, women are expected to walk a difficult tightrope—if we have strong views, we can be labeled emotional, yet, if we have a subtle approach, we can be labeled weak or ineffective. This paradox will often leave women feeling confused and undervalued in their profession.

Women in the workplace know this: God loves you and

has designed you for a purpose—His purpose. He has also set before and around you a legion of like-minded women who have faced similar struggles, celebrations, and circumstances, and are willing to share with you their wisdom and advice. As you spend part of each day with this devotional, I pray that you feel enriched, encouraged, and deeply loved with each testimony you read.

> "The LORD your God is with you, the Mighty Warrior who saves. He will take great delight in you; in his love he will no longer rebuke you, but will rejoice over you with singing." —Zephaniah 3:17

Cheryl Bachelder
Former CEO of Popeyes® Louisiana Kitchen, Inc.
Named the world's top CEO by *Inc.* magazine (June 8, 2017)
Author of *Dare to Serve: How to Drive Superior Results by Serving Others*

Foreword

By Sharron E. Hudson

*T*he most influential women in my life were my mom, Mary, and her mom, Gramma Dover. Both were working-women outside (and inside) the home. I used to go to work with my mom, and she taught me how to count money, file papers, and perform other tasks she thought would be useful in my learning process. Gramma taught me how to bake and I watched her sew. I learned from my Gramma's story that during WWII she worked in a factory and was also a taxi driver! Both of these strong, caring, influential women in my life are with the Lord now—I miss being with them.

Growing up in The Salvation Army, it wasn't unusual for me to see a woman speaking from the pulpit, teaching a Sunday school class, driving a van, and working in an office. Besides my mom and Gramma, women Salvation Army officers (ordained ministers) taught me to have confidence in myself and to "serve the Lord with gladness."

All of these special women in my life would have appreciated this devotional for women by women. Take time out of your busy schedule to breathe in God's Word and find rest for your soul.

Commissioner Sharron E. Hudson
National President of Women's Ministries for The Salvation Army (USA National Headquarters, Alexandria, VA)

Dear Searchers of Refreshment,

When I was on the Global Executive teams of two Fortune 500 companies and one Fortune 1000 company, serving at work, prioritizing the relationship with my husband and our four children in a blended family, and keeping my relationship with God as the center of my life, was a daily challenge. Being in community with other women living the same dimensions of "Work, Love, Pray" helped me navigate each day.

4wordwomen.org was created so real, passionate, faithful women can be in community with other like-minded women. Our dream at 4word is to create a Global Community of Christian Women in the Workplace who encourages each other to be BOLD in every aspect of our lives.

We wrote *Be Refreshed* to give you a short, impactful devotional with which to start each day and to encourage you in your God-given calling. Start anytime and complete the book at your own pace. We know time is a precious commodity in your busy life, so we designed each devotional entry to be a quick, yet refreshing, addition to your day. After five days of devotional entries, we've included a time of reflection for you, complete with questions and a prayer. Our hope is that this gives you time to pause and find a few moments of peace and clarity.

It's time to lay down the guilt and embrace joy! May

this devotional refresh you as you face challenges and seize the opportunities He places before you!

Diane Paddison
Founder of 4word women
Former Executive Team at Trammell Crow Company, CBRE, and ProLogis

Week 1

Broken World

*"My Presence will go with you,
and I will give you rest."*

Exodus 33:14

I've seen many smart and talented women "burn out" of their professional careers. They leave their jobs not because they feel called to something else, but because they're tired and fed up.

No matter what you accomplish at work, no matter how smart, capable, or eager you are, no matter how loving your husband is, or well-behaved your kids are, the world you live in is broken. You'll experience betrayal and disappointment, embarrassment and failure. Your salary and job title can't offer you much in those instances, but faith will sustain you and guide you if you let it. Let faith permeate your life, and build your career from there.

You need faith first, because the rewards, accolades, and benefits that come from work alone cannot sustain you. God's calling is the purpose and inspiration that will never fade.

Diane Paddison
Founder of 4word women
Former Executive Team at Trammell Crow Company, CBRE, and ProLogis

Daily Bread

What does the Lord require of you? To act justly
and to love mercy and to walk humbly with your God.

Micah 6:8

"Work" and "home" each offer me refreshment from the other. Just managing breakfast and getting small people dressed is a marathon. I'm usually pretty relieved to have some space at work to use different skills and talk with different people. But then at the end of the day, I'm tired of spreadsheets and office frustrations and ready for giggles, wrestling, snuggles, and books. I enjoy having both worlds. Knowing the "other one" is waiting for me keeps me focused on the one I'm in.

Ask God for your daily bread: enough grace for the moment with either your children or your colleagues, enough attention to do a good job on the task at-hand, enough humor to roll with the punches, and enough dependence on God to love the people He's put into your life with His love.

Elizabeth Knox
Author of *Faith Powered Profession*
Founder of MatchPace

Prayer Partner

Trust in the Lord with all your heart and lean not on
your own understanding; in all your ways submit to him,
and he will make your paths straight.

Proverbs 3:5–6

*A*fter the sale of our company and a rewarding career in business, I was ready to implement my plan to really study the Bible, join community boards to give back, enjoy my family, and travel. But God knew I had struggles ahead and that I wasn't prepared.

To prepare me, Jesus blessed me with a growing relationship with Him through disciplined Bible study, prayer, strong spiritual leaders, and a loving husband as my prayer partner. Christ clearly gave me the strength to face these last two years of serious family strife, financial losses, my sister's untimely death, and the death of three precious friends. In Him, I have peace. I know how much I need Him.

Ka Cotter
Former Vice Chair, The Staubach Company
4word Advisory Board Member

Radical Giving

Each of you should give what you have decided in
your heart to give, not reluctantly or under compulsion,
for God loves a cheerful giver.

2 Corinthians 9:7

Radical givers hold everything they have (their time, talent, and treasure) with open hands. They believe everything they have belongs to God and they are His stewards. They seek His leading in how to use what He's entrusted to them.

When we remember God owns everything, we realize He doesn't need anything from us. Yet He allows us to co-labor with Him. We *get* to give! If we open our eyes, we can see unmet needs all around us. We get to be a part of the miracles produced by life-changing generosity!

God's economy makes no sense. We cannot out-give God. Giving fills me with overwhelming joy, peace, and freedom. It *really* is more blessed to give than to receive. The life of generosity is a journey and a grand adventure.

Lacie Stevens
Coauthor of *God Calling*
On staff with Generous Giving

Love Him First

Jesus replied: "Love the Lord your God with all your heart and with all your soul and with all your mind."

Matthew 22:37

*W*e all have the same amount of time. Some squander it, give it to the wrong people, or feel guilty about it every day. Most of us don't think we'll ever have enough of it.

We're busy women. We've read the books, tried the apps, and could teach others a thing or two about time management. So why is the guilt always there? Is it because we're trying to please too many people?

There will never be enough of us to go around. The most important thing we can do is honor God with how we spend this precious commodity. Ask God: "What does it look like to love you first with my time? How can I say yes to time with my spouse? What is your will for the right rhythm for my life?"

Lori Berry, MA-PC
Pastoral Counselor
4word Advisory Board Member

REFLECT & REFRESH

How did you make your relationship with God a priority this week?

Which areas of your life do you need to rethink against God's priorities?

Are you a good steward of the time God has granted you? Why or why not?

Lord, open my eyes to see where my scales of time are dangling off-balance. Help me to understand that my way and my schedule are not always your way and your schedule. Show me how to be a good steward of all with which you have blessed me, but most importantly, give me the discipline to make my faith first.

Week 2

The Plenty

I have learned to be content
whatever the circumstances.

Philippians 4:11

My first temporary office was an under-stairway broom closet. Despite the lack of air and constant overhead rumble, I was thrilled and thankful to work in a major bank, knowing we'd soon move to the new high-rise headquarters. But once settled into my beautiful new office, the daily joy of my close colleagues sharing our toaster and coffee maker evaporated. Shouldn't we be even happier? Wasn't this what I deserved as a young and talented professional banker? What a godly lesson as to what's really important.

My prayer is that Jesus will help me remember to enjoy, but not need, the things of this world—both in my work life and home life. The "plenty," comprised of career success and respect, are gifts from Him, but the times of "less" remind me to lean into Him for true contentment and peace. Whatever the circumstances, they can bring me closer to Him.

Patricia Myers
Former Director, Talent Management
Director, Leadership Development for National Commercial
Bank of Saudi Arabia (NCB)
Executive Coach and 4word Board Member

Christian Irony

The prayer of a righteous person
is powerful and effective.

James 5:16

"*W*ell, I guess all we can do is pray." These words have come from my lips. The irony of this statement as a Christian is embarrassing.

James 5:16–18 discusses how Elijah was human, just like you and me. He didn't have special powers or some secret handshake with God. Elijah simply prayed earnestly to stop the rain, and for three years, it stopped. Wow!

James 5:13 says, "Is anyone among you in trouble? Let them pray. Is anyone happy? Let them sing songs of praise." This reminds me of how my husband and I send texts back and forth throughout the day, like "Hi," "Miss you," or "I'm craving guacamole." You know, the usual stuff. We do this because we want to be closer. I imagine God sees it the same way; He loves us and desires a relationship with us! Prayer is an integral part of that relationship.

Sandra Crawford Williamson
CEO of Crawford Creative Consulting
4word Advisory Board Member

Your Rhythm

For if, while we were God's enemies,
we were reconciled to him through the death of his Son,
how much more, having been reconciled,
shall we be saved through his life!

Romans 5:10

God designed each one of us for friendship. Yet many of us suffer the pain of loneliness, chaos, or all-out war when it comes to our relationships. True peace and rest will only come when our number one friendship is with Jesus. When we accept this gift of friendship and follow Him daily, our relationships with others begin to reflect the peace that God intends.

To truly glean all God has for us, we must understand the Big Picture. As we grow and mature in our relationship with Christ, we grow in understanding God's plans. As we love and follow His design, we find ourselves experiencing the best life … the life we were designed to live, filled with the rhythm of hard work, loving relationships, and peaceful rest.

Susan Thomas
Licensed Professional Counselor
Senior Pastor's Wife, Keystone Church

Invest in Others

Therefore, since we are surrounded by such a great cloud of witnesses, let us throw off everything that hinders and the sin that so easily entangles. And let us run with perseverance the race marked out for us.

Hebrews 12:1

I believe mentoring is my spiritual gift. Investing in others through mentorship is a way for me to give back. It's easy to give of myself in that way, and I get so much in return. I learn from each person I talk to and spend time with. We all go through trials, changes, and opportunities, and often evaluate what to do based on someone else's experiences. It's a blessing to be able to be that person.

Do you want to share your life experiences in a positive way? If so, then mentoring could be for you. Pray about your role as a mentor. The opportunity to bless someone else will also result in a blessing for you!

Tanya Hart Little
Founder and CEO of Hart Advisors Group, Hart Commercial, and VistaPointe Partners

Short Life

But even if you should suffer for what is right,
you are blessed. "Do not fear their threats;
do not be frightened."

1 Peter 3:14

When my husband and I married, he was a widower with four daughters in their early to late twenties. When I met the girls, they were still grieving. It took a long time for us to get comfortable with each other.

As women, we tend to take everything personally, which I did at the beginning. I thought, "Why am I not bonding with these young women?" The fact is, they were strangers when I first met them, as was I to them.

Everyone is going to be challenged during this life, regardless of our circumstances. At the end of the day, if you serve others and just be kind, your life will be so much more enriched. Life is short. Making a positive impact at the end of the day is what we should all strive toward.

Shivaun Palmer
Founder and CEO, Plaid for Women, Inc.

REFLECT & REFRESH

What was your relationship "highlight" this week?
(Spouse, family, friend, etc.)

Thinking back through your week, were there any
missed opportunities to begin or nurture a relationship
in your life?

Have you brought any relationships to God in prayer this
week? If so, has your prayer been answered?

Lord, I want to be the best example of you and
your unfailing love. Give me opportunities to be
your hands, your feet, and your voice. Guide me
to relationships that will not only edify me but
glorify you. When life seems to be stretching me
to the point of breaking, grant me the relief of
friendship. When life unfolds blessing after blessing, remind me to turn to those around me and be
a source of love and joy.

Week 3

Empty Gesture

Do your best to present yourself to God as one approved, a worker who does not need to be ashamed and who correctly handles the word of truth.

2 Timothy 2:15

There's no such thing as an empty gesture when we recognize we're objects of God's choosing. Following His prompt to action is like tossing a stone into a still pool. Once it touches water, little can be done to control the resulting ripples.

God's Plan A is using the likes of ordinary you and me in joining Him in His extraordinary activity in the world. Some of God's best work is using those no one would expect to be of use and infusing them and their actions with His power. It's one of the hallmarks of His handiwork, using persons often overlooked to serve as leading players in His mission across the planet.

Will today be the day you initiate a ripple? It begins with just one. Any one of us can be that one.

Steve Haas
Catalyst—World Vision

Heavy Life

I consider that our present sufferings are not worth
comparing with the glory that will be revealed in us.

Romans 8:18

My daughter suffers from a debilitating medical condition. She's been incredibly brave and resilient, but
watching her in pain, seeing her spirits sink with each new
diagnosis or failed treatment, weighs on me. I pray constantly for healing, and I pray that I could take her place.

In this season, I look to the example of Harriet Beecher
Stowe. She was a woman guided by her faith, a devoted
wife, a mother, and an incredibly successful professional.
Then she lost her young son to cholera. She was overwhelmed, but she kept moving toward God. So many
people turn away from God when their suffering is great or
protracted, but not Harriet.

If you're in the midst of a difficult time, I hope that like
me, you can take comfort from Harriet's example

Diane Paddison
Founder of 4word women
Former Executive Team at Trammell Crow Company,
CBRE, and ProLogis

Need to Control

"Very truly I tell you, whoever believes in me will do the works I have been doing, and they will do even greater things than these, because I am going to the Father."

John 14:12

I'm a control freak of the highest order. God has done a great work to temper my natural tendency to want to control things, for which I'm very grateful. There's no better example of this tempering than my struggle with infertility. I spent many years struggling, trying to put God on my timetable. It was only in my complete surrender and willingness to get out of the way—so that I could actually listen and hear what God was saying—that I experienced true guidance and direction.

If you let go, God can work miracles through your trials and tribulations. Give Him the trust He deserves and craves from you, and prepare to be left in awe with what He accomplishes through your surrender.

Rebecca Henderson
Clothe Me Co-Op Coordinator

Soaring Eagle

Those who hope in the Lord will renew their strength.
They will soar on wings like eagles.

Isaiah 40:31

*E*agles make it look so easy to soar over the cliff from their lofty nest. But it's a complex operation. They rely on currents (which are thermal winds moving straight from earth toward heaven), which means waiting, learning about timing, and trusting the power of the current. When I look at the steps it takes to fly, I can see how they hold great lessons for us.

First, there's *flapping*, staying in constant motion. It may seem awkward and takes lots of energy. (Gracefulness, however, isn't required!) Next comes *gliding*, where we coast and build speed. Gravity can help move this along. (A leap of faith?) But gliding can't last forever. We need to keep learning and improve this ability whenever possible.

Finally, there's *soaring*. Here strong wings capable of catching an unseen current are required. I thank God that He's given me the ability to soar in Him.

Lisa Creed
Owner of Good News Coaching

Faith Journey

I will instruct you and teach you in the way you
should go; I will counsel you with my loving eye on you.

Psalm 32:8

I walked back to my office in disbelief. Were they serious? They really wanted me to move to Qatar? Most people can barely pronounce the name, if they even know it exists.

At the time, I was teaching a Bible study about Abraham's faith and his unexpected request from God to move to a foreign land. He had no idea where he was going, but he obeyed. At least I knew where I was going. I had to trust that God had me in His hands. A Christian, single, American girl in the Middle East ... as a leader. Picture that!

I have to admit this was the most awe-inspiring journey I have ever taken. My faith and prayer life were taken to another level, all because I let go and let God.

Kathy F. Belton
Execution Planning Manager with ExxonMobil
Research & Engineering Company

REFLECT & REFRESH

What is one obstacle in your life keeping you from surrendering to God's calling today?

What stage of "taking flight" are you in today: flapping, gliding, or soaring? What is one area that strengthens your faith?

How can you make space in your day to watch for an opportunity to initiate a "ripple" as God prompts you to action?

Lord, help me let go of my desire to control my life. Help me trust you in the face of temptation, illness, and any other obstacles that may get in the way of following your plan. Teach me to wait on your timing and trust the current as I gain the strength to soar. And when you ask me to take a leap of faith, help me to make the jump without hesitation. Use the seemingly ordinary moments in my day to do your extraordinary activity in the world, creating ripples that reach far beyond all I could ever ask or imagine.

Week 4

Barren

"'Sir,' the man replied, 'leave it alone for one more year, and I'll dig around it and fertilize it. If it bears fruit next year, fine! If not, then cut it down.'"

Luke 13:8–9

There are so many times we want to simply give up, on ourselves, our lives, our work ... perhaps even on others who are important in our lives.

"The Parable of the Barren Fig Tree" describes how, even after two years of what may seem like "no progress," the Lord encourages us to "give it just one more year." If we continue to nurture ourselves, or others, there's hope that God's will may become more apparent, and that the tree may indeed bear fruit.

The Lord is patient with us, even on those days when we seem "lost." Perhaps we can demonstrate the same patience with ourselves and others. Imagine the joy of fruit on what was once a barren tree!

Evelyn M. Lee, PhD
Founder of Vocation Catalyst, Ltd.

Your Surroundings

Praise be to the God and Father of our Lord Jesus Christ, the Father of compassion and the God of all comfort, who comforts us in all our troubles, so that we can comfort those in any trouble with the comfort we ourselves receive from God.

2 Corinthians 1:3-4

*M*y life looks nothing like I thought it would. Although God has allowed me to travel a road I wouldn't have chosen, I wouldn't trade it, because I've seen Him at work. Whenever I felt overwhelmed along the way, prayerful friends continually pointed me back to the Lord.

Surround yourself with friends who remind you of God's truth and walk with you in hard times. Be vulnerable with a few people who know your whole story. Get in the trenches with others as they experience troubles. God never wastes our suffering. Whatever you've experienced can be used by Him to comfort and support one another. Let Him use you to bless others, as you've been blessed!

Denny Slaton
Stewardship Advisor for Seed Effect

Crucial Waiting

Be patient, then, brothers and sisters,
until the Lord's coming. See how the farmer
waits for the land to yield its valuable crop,
patiently waiting for the autumn and spring rains.

James 5:7

Need to make a big decision?

First, pray. Then, wait. Waiting is crucial. In my life, I've learned that plunging into situations without much forethought usually wreaks havoc on the good plans that were prepared in advance for me. As I've gotten older, I understand that prayerfully seeking and waiting reaps greater rewards. Sometimes, *waiting* means stepping back and giving a question or idea a few days of space. Other times, waiting can be as simple as taking a long, slow breath. Take that time of waiting and use it to open your heart and mind to God.

When I wait with a listening heart, I see God work in creative and unexpected ways.

Dawn Atwood
Sales Director for Jay Franco and Sons

Work's Purpose

So God created mankind in his own image, in the image
of God he created them male and female he created
them. God blessed them and said to them, 'Be fruitful
and increase in number; fill the earth and subdue it. Rule
over the fish in the sea and the birds in the sky and over
every living creature that moves on the ground.

Genesis 1:27-28

"*Y*ou don't get meaning from your work; you bring
meaning to your work." I first heard that phrase in a
sermon years ago at our church, and it really struck a chord
with me. I realized I had been searching for "meaningful"
work rather than understanding that all work is important
to God. To better understand God's purpose for business
in this world, I began asking myself how my daily work
honored God and others.

I had to go all the way back to Genesis 1:27–28 to be
reminded that we were actually created to participate in God's
agenda for this world. Eventually I realized I had begun to
think of my work primarily as a means to make a living while
I served God elsewhere. If the place I spent the majority of
my time wasn't important to God, then what was?

Begin to look at your work from God's point of view
and learn how to honor Him and others through it.

Bonnie Wurzbacher
Chief Resource Development Officer, World Vision International

Refuge

So that your faith might not rest on human wisdom,
but on God's power.

1 Corinthians 2:5

*W*ho is a refugee?

Amidst our many blessings, it's hard to grapple with the thought of a child without a home, family, or nation. As a young woman, faith came to feel like a repetitive action—an obligation driven by guilt or fear. But for my husband, Lopez Lomong, faith was a beacon during his childhood struggle as he ran from fear to freedom. For him, spirituality was the warmth of a mother's hug and the prayer to survive the trials of civil war.

I saw faith in a whole new light as I became part of Lopez's journey to become an Olympic athlete. From a "Lost Boy" (a Sudanese refugee) came a profound testament of faith and purpose. I came to know God's strength as a smile in spite of trauma, perseverance through pain and loss, and unfailing determination. In faith and love, we all find refuge.

Brittany Lomong Morreale
Captain, USAF
Wife of two-time Olympian, Lopez Lomong

REFLECT & REFRESH

Does your life look how you thought it would? Is God asking you to persevere as you wait on His timing and blessing?

In what ways have you been relying on human wisdom instead of God's wisdom? What steps can you take today to change your perspective and seek God's wisdom first?

In the midst of busy days and long to-do lists, how can you create margin in your day and allow God the opportunity to speak to you?

Lord, as I face a busy day with a long to-do list, help me create margin in my days, even carving out just a few minutes of time each morning to seek you first. Help me rely on your power to accomplish the tasks that fill each day and ignore the wisdom of the world that tells me I need to do more and be more in order to be worthy and loved. Give me a listening heart and the patience to wait on your timing.

Week 5

Just Show Up

"I am sending you out like sheep among wolves.
Therefore be as shrewd as snakes
and as innocent as doves."

Matthew 10:16

*O*verall church attendance is on a spiral decline. The harsh reality is if we don't change our approach to the gospel, our legacy of faith will be lost. The boardroom is our new pulpit (or at least it should be), and God has called women and men to live out their faith within this context.

I believe each person is unique, and there's no single, right way to approach evangelism. We simply need to be sensitive to the Holy Spirit, rather than follow a one-size-fits-all approach. With a high regard for relationships and an authentic spirit, there's ample opportunity to connect on a spiritual level with our colleagues and clients.

It's as simple as that. There's nothing weird, tricky, or inappropriate about it. We simply need to show up. End of story. Or shall I say a beginning of a new story?

Alana Walker Carpenter
CEO of Intriciti

His Favor

"The Lord bless you and keep you; the Lord make
his face shine on you and be gracious to you;
the Lord turn his face toward you and give you peace.

Numbers 6:24-26

I have three children: two teenagers at home and a college student. My son David is at Duke University. The transition has been tough, as we're a very close family. A friend assured me that soon we'd rejoice in our new relationship with each child more than we'd mourn the loss of our previous life.

Though it's a process, I'm starting to experience this. Despite the distance, God shines His face upon us when we miss our son. God is gracious to let us experience the joy of being together and helps us find creative ways to stay connected when we're apart. Through it all, God fills us with peace, for His love binds the five of us together every moment—through the wonderful gift of prayer.

Amaryllis Sánchez Wohlever, MD
Author of *Walking with Jesus in Healthcare*

Not Immune

The Lord is my strength and my song.

Psalm 118:14 NKJV

*N*one of us are immune to health challenges, whether they are personal or affect someone close to us. A major health crisis can threaten to throw the balance off in every area of our life, consuming our time, energy, and faith. Is it possible to carve out time for rest?

If you're a caregiver, there are five "musts" of rest you need to introduce into your life. First, start each morning with prayer to center your day and set your priorities. Second, stay in God's Word. Third, surround yourself with support. Fourth, take care of yourself, because if you aren't taking care of yourself, how can you, in turn, care for others? Finally, be intentional about time with your spouse.

Above all, don't stop praying for God's healing and for His purposes to be fulfilled through the battle.

Diane Paddison
Founder of 4word women
Former Executive Team at Trammell Crow Company, CBRE, and ProLogis

Call on Grace

These words that I command you today shall be on your heart. You shall teach them diligently to your children, and shall talk of them when you sit in your house.

Deuteronomy 6:6–7 ESV

My husband and I pray with our kids, for our kids, in front of our kids, and around our kids. We take them to church, keep them involved in youth group, and surround them with Christian friends and great worship music.

But what have we done to foster our kids' spiritual development that will help them through a crisis? I realize what really matters is not just the practice, it's in the presence. My children know how to vulnerably pour out their hearts to God and invite Him to take control.

Our kids have learned how to face trials by watching their parents go through tough times, completely spent and laid out before God, calling on His grace. Then, they see the joy.

Lori Berry, MA-PC
Pastoral Counselor
4word women Advisory Board Member

Space for Grace

God is able to make all grace abound to you,
so that having all sufficiency in all things at all times,
you may abound in every good work.

2 Corinthians 9:8 ESV

*G*uilt weighs us down when we don't forgive ourselves for things we've done—or haven't done. There are times when this "tape" plays over and over, and the process of forgiving (and forgetting!) seems out of reach.

A friend recently described a place of prayer as a "space for grace." She spoke of this concept as opening a safe encounter with a merciful God. We can expand the "space for grace" to include times when we gather with others in prayer, listen to a friend, or give ourselves a break. By keeping company with Christ, we learn the unforced rhythms of grace, allowing us to live freely and lightly.

Where can you give yourself space for grace today? Wherever it is, begin the journey of releasing your guilt and keeping company with Christ.

Carol Seiler
Commissioner, The Salvation Army

REFLECT & REFRESH

Who do you need to "show up for" today at work, at home, or in your community?

Are you setting a good example of prayerfulness for your children, spouse, friends or coworkers?

What steps can you take today to establish or maintain a consistent time of prayer each day?

Lord, today I commit to taking moments throughout my day to stop what I'm doing and come to you in prayer. Help me remember that without prayer, I cannot fulfill the calling you have given me to be your hands and feet at work and at home. May I always seek to set an example of prayerfulness and humility for those around me, and give myself grace when I let the cares of the world crowd out my time spent with you in prayer.

Week 6

Reinforcement

You believe that there is one God. Good!
Even the demons believe that—and shudder.

James 2:19

*F*aith is the key foundation of my life. It is part of my core being. As a Christian, my goal is to glorify God in all I do each and every day. This is foundational in my personal/family life and my work life. I take time to pray for my family and friends every day, and my work family as well. I believe if we obey the Word of God completely, He will provide the ability to handle any situation we may face in life.

If you're struggling to keep your faith as your foundation, it's time to seek God. Dedicate a time every day that you turn off the noise and distractions of the world and instead focus on your heavenly Father. Setting aside this time will not only reinforce your foundation, it will also begin enriching the rest of your life.

Ellen Barker
SVP, CIO Texas Instruments

Effective Evangelism

Always be prepared to give an answer to everyone who asks you to give the reason for the hope that you have. But do this with gentleness and respect.

1 Peter 3:15

There are many common misconceptions about witnessing. One is that you have to tell people the whole story all at once, then they must make a commitment immediately. *Only* if that happens have you evangelized. Good evangelism, like good wine, takes time. Give people little bits of truth to ponder. When we do this we raise curiosity, not dampen it.

Another misconception is that if you keep talking, you'll convince people. Talk less, live and love people more—like Jesus. Your silence will preach the message!

You can try to convince people of a message, or you can give people the experience of God's grace. If God gives you an opportunity to evangelize, He will give you the right words and actions to see it through.

John Leonard, PhD
Pastor of Cresheim Valley Church in Philadelphia, PA

12 Steps

All have sinned and fall short of the glory of God,

Romans 3:23 NASB

When the Christian community learns that transparency is the key to healing, that God made us to be there for one another and share His hope and love, we'll discover what "bottom line" love is really about. We all know we're not perfect, but everyone is afraid to talk about it.

God has prepared me to be open and honest about my past. After going through the process of writing my book, I realized that the time I spent in a Twelve Step Program (when I got sober thirty years ago) was where I learned to get up in front of a podium and tell my story. It never occurred to me that was what I was doing.

Learn to say what you need to say. It's really the most effective form of communication. Focus on what will count in the long run. It's a very freeing place to be!

Julie Ziglar Norman
Keynote speaker, Author, Coach, and Daughter of Zig Ziglar

Being Genuine

Do not let any unwholesome talk come
out of your mouths, but only what is helpful
for building others up according to their needs,
that it may benefit those who listen.

Ephesians 4:29

*H*ow nice is *too* nice? The answer is simple: You're being too nice when you stop being genuine. People who are nice without authenticity are like annoying sales people complimenting us to close the sale.

Maintaining a genuine positive attitude, and encouraging and complimenting coworkers authentically, can help us strike the perfect balance between "too tough" and "too nice."

Transforming frustrations into a positive attitude at work is one way of sharing the gospel with our coworkers. Maybe we'll be accused of being "too nice." But if we focus on fulfilling the role God has given each of us, the impact we'll make on those around us will go far beyond closing a big sale or achieving the next milestone at work.

Diane Paddison
Founder of 4word women
Former Executive Team at Trammell Crow Company,
CBRE, and ProLogis

God of Order

Then Jesus declared, "I am the bread of life.
Whoever comes to me will never go hungry,
and whoever believes in me will never be thirsty."

John 6:35

*G*od is a God of order. He created the earth in six specific days in a purposeful manner.

When you make a plan, it should be a complete plan and include relationship(s), vocation, health, education, recreation, and service. We are to grow in the fruit of the Spirit and be more Christlike. The more fruit we have, the more attractive we are. And the more attractive we are, the more influence we have to illuminate a path for non-believers and to encourage and edify fellow believers.

Do I demonstrate love, joy, peace, patience, kindness, goodness, faithfulness, gentleness, and self-control? The more I radiate the fruit of the Spirit, the more Christlike I am becoming, which is God's ultimate plan for my life.

Kelly McDermott Thurman
Former Global Head of Sales for EDS
Managing Partner, AdviSoar
4word Chair of the Board

REFLECT & REFRESH

Do you find it difficult to be transparent about the things you're struggling with? Is there an area of your life you could be more open and honest about in order to let God minister through you?

Have you struggled to find the balance between "too tough" and "too nice" at work? Find an opportunity to encourage or authentically compliment a coworker, friend, or family member today.

Which fruit of the Spirit—love, joy, peace, patience, kindness, goodness, faithfulness, gentleness, or self-control— do you struggle to emulate the most? What steps can you take to exhibit the fruit of the Spirit at work and at home?

Lord, show me how I can be more transparent, humbly sharing both the good and the bad in my life with coworkers, friends, and family. Help me authentically share my faith with those I meet each day. When others wrong me, help me stay positive and display your character, so they can see and know you through me.

Week 7

Subplots

Glorify the Lord with me;
let us exalt his name together.

Psalm 34:3

I've always been an independent person, so God taught
me a lesson on dependence that began when I moved
to Germany. While rock climbing with friends, I fell from
the top of the rock wall, broke two vertebrae, and was
rushed to emergency surgery. After the operation, the sur-
geon told my friends I only had a 1 percent chance of
walking again.

I do my best to live each day as a light. I praise God that
His light transcends language barriers, while also sharing
with as many others the good works God is doing in my
body. A friend once told me she was grateful "her subplot
in God's story overlapped with my subplot." I love that
analogy. I used to be terrified that my life was just a supporting role in someone else's life. Since then, I've come
to realize what a gift it is to be a minor character in God's
story.

Laura Hewett
Bible Teacher

Reach Up

Remember your leaders, who spoke
the word of God to you. Consider the outcome
of their way of life and imitate their faith.

Hebrews 13:7

*A*sk any woman who's traversed the winding path of career, family, and faith, and she's sure to express how she wouldn't be where she is today without the help of women who walked ahead of her.

After my divorce, I needed women around to encourage me and lift me up. God blessed me with a dear friend who gave me the confidence to take the next step forward each day. She encouraged me to continue to "be like Christ" and set an example for my kids.

I cannot stress enough the importance of having older women in our lives to "reach up" to on a regular basis. That way when trials come—and they will—we can lean on them for Christlike love and support to help carry us through.

Diane Paddison
Founder of 4word women
Former Executive Team at Trammell Crow Company,
CBRE, and ProLogis

True Sacrifice

Submit yourselves, then, to God.
Resist the devil, and he will flee from you.

James 4:7

I've known for years that food was a big issue for me. I was also aware that food could be an addiction and idol. But because of convenience—and my love of food—I chose to ignore this for quite some time. I tried dieting, but would always gain the weight back and more. I listened to the negative self-talk that said, "You're going to fail in the end, so why even try?"

God slowly convicted me that I needed to care for my body, because it was His temple. While He can use us wherever we are in life, I felt like I could be of more service to Him if I was healthy. I knew a true sacrifice and lifestyle change was going to be the only way to get healthy permanently.

What do you need to sacrifice today? What's God calling you to lay before Him?

Lisa Kilgore
Healthy and Humbled Child of God

Jesus Standard Time

"Come, follow me," Jesus said,
"and I will send you out to fish for people."

Matthew 4:19

I consider myself an excellent time manager. I plan things in advance, artfully maneuver our family's schedule, work full-time, and volunteer for our church and community. Yet there've been many times where my priorities have been called out for being way off track.

Jesus was an excellent example of how to make the most of your time. Jesus delegated tasks, made time for friends, and took time to grieve with his buddies, Mary and Martha, before raising their brother Lazarus from the dead. Jesus recognized the human body's needs. He knew when it was time to recharge and connect with His Father. Remember, if Jesus did it, it's important.

What if we all prayed, "Jesus, take my schedule and have your way with it." How well we'd manage time if we prayed like that! We might just be on Jesus Standard Time!

Lori Berry, MA-PC
Pastoral Counselor
4word Advisory Board Member

Vulnerable

As Solomon grew old, his wives turned his heart after other gods, and his heart was not fully devoted to the Lord his God, as the heart of David his father had been.

1 Kings 11:4

Solomon has always fascinated me. As a novice, he was humble and wise enough to seek wisdom above all else. Later in life, Solomon was steeped in idol worship. The phrase repeated throughout 1 Kings 11 is that Solomon's heart had turned away from God.

What's drawing your love? We can attend church and have a daily Quiet Time, while the affection of our heart is turning toward something/someone else. When our heart is no longer turning toward the Lord, we're vulnerable to compromise.

All of us need to continually ask the Lord, "What have I started to love above you?" The heart will always be after something. It's only through intimacy, with a heart truly seeking the Lord, that we can finish well.

Shannan Crawford, PsyD
Licensed Psychologist
CEO of Dr. Crawford & Associates, PLLC

REFLECT & REFRESH

How can you reorganize your priorities and your to-do list, so that you're living on "Jesus Standard Time"?

Ask God to reveal any hidden or stubborn idols in your life. Commit to laying them aside and putting Him first.

Is there a woman you can "reach up to" and ask for wisdom and accountability? Take a bold step and ask her for a few minutes of her time. Continue to invest in relationships that help you put God first.

Lord, thank you for giving me examples of wisdom and godly living to help keep me focused on you and your will for my life. Show me the things that have become idols in my life, taking my attention, love, and worship away from you. Give me guardrails in my life in the form of mentors and friends who can help me identify idols and keep me accountable, as I seek to put you first.

Week 8

Be More Supportive

Therefore, as God's chosen people, holy and dearly
loved, clothe yourselves with compassion, kindness,
humility, gentleness and patience.

Colossians 3:12

When I became a mother, I became painfully aware of how unaccommodating I may have been with working mothers earlier in my career.

So how can we be more supportive of working mothers? 1) Have a set time for the end of the workday. 2) Be mindful of the times meetings are set and give advanced notice. 3) Keep in mind the "second shift." Allow more flexibility in the workday, enabling parents to get work done after the kids are in bed. 4) Be understanding when business travel is involved. 5) Set your company culture to value and reward results, not face time or time in the chair.

Study after study shows that firms have better results—and happier, healthier, and more loyal employees—when we offer flexible opportunities. Let's strive to be flexible with everyone, in and out of work!

Sandra Crawford Williamson
CEO of Crawford Creative Consulting
4word Advisory Board Member

Vessel For Comfort

Lord, be gracious to us; we long for you. Be our strength
every morning, our salvation in time of distress.

Isaiah 33:2

God has been evident in every step of my journey to
parenthood and beyond. From the outset, He prepared
my husband's heart and mine by leading us to embryo
adoption the day before we received the fateful infertility
diagnosis. Instead of being caught off guard when the doctor said, "Kelli's eggs are no longer viable," we arrived at the
appointment armed with questions and filled with peace.

God used the pain, uncertainty, and joys we've experienced in ways we could have never imagined. We're
constantly reminded of His goodness, provision, and faithfulness in our lives, as we've shared our infertility and
embryo adoption journey with others.

If you're facing an uncertain situation, take comfort
in knowing that God may be grooming you to become a
vessel for spreading comfort and understanding to those
who'll come behind you. What a blessing!

Kelli Gassman
Christ-follower, Wife, Mommy, Professor,
and Marketing Professional

Salute to Single Moms

"The rain came down, the streams rose, and the winds blew and beat against that house; yet it did not fall, because it had its foundation on the rock."

Matthew 7:25

*M*y time as a single working mom was truly a time of growth and trusting in God for my strength! Single moms don't have the extreme blessing of having a spouse with whom to share the load of parenting, so they often hold immeasurable amounts of responsibilities on their shoulders just to get themselves and their families through each day.

Single working moms, I salute you. I know the daily struggles you face, and I know the sacrifices you make for the sake of your families. Don't be afraid to accept help when it's offered; it doesn't make you any less amazing as a person and mother. Continuously seek strength from your heavenly Father and trust He'll see you and your loved ones through every day.

Diane Paddison
Founder of 4word women
Former Executive Team at Trammell Crow Company, CBRE, and ProLogis

Better Together

All of you, have unity of mind, sympathy, brotherly love,
a tender heart, and a humble mind.

1 Peter 3:8 ESV

*T*rauma and loss affect us negatively if we keep them inside, and spending too much time on social media doesn't help. We see the picture-perfect posts of those around us and silently compare our real lives with the highlight reel others are sharing. It doesn't help that the church, as a whole, has not historically fostered authenticity. It's easy to feel like we're expected to wear our nicest clothes and put on our prettiest smile just to walk in the door.

Things can easily begin to spiral downward when we start rehearsing stories in our minds that tell us we can't show our true selves, because we simply aren't good enough. By intentionally fostering authentic relationships, focusing on truth, and supporting each other on the journey, we're reminded of God's great love for us and how He created us to thrive in community.

Crystal Gornto

Founder and Chief Love Amplifier at HeartStories

Unity through Community

How good and pleasant it is when
God's people live together in unity!

Psalm 133:1

To us, "community" is a support system. We imagine it being a pot that you both add to and take out of. Community is honest, real, dirty, authentic, and it grows. It means having people in your life that you learn from, look up to, and are challenged by—but whom you can also mentor and teach. An "iron sharpens iron" (Proverbs 27:17) relationship is what we look for in our community. We believe that a group that shares the reassuring knowledge of God's goodness, but is not afraid to bring up their challenging questions of faith, defines a healthy community.

We try to surround ourselves with people who are much stronger and smarter in their faith than us. Shared experiences can help unify a community. In order for a community to be healthy, there needs to be a diverse group of believers, united by a common belief, goal, or experience.

April Swaine and Jana Ventura
Business Operations Manager & Human Resources
at Practec LLC
Graduate Recruitment Manager, UK & South Europe, Amazon

REFLECT & REFRESH

Are you part of an "honest, real, dirty, authentic" community? How can you find or invest in a support system?

What is one thing you can do to support a single mom in your life today?

Challenge yourself to ask for help once today, whether the "ask" is big or small.

> Lord, help me to lay aside my tendency to put on a pretty face, afraid to show my true self to those around me. Thank you for the women who have gone before me, helping me navigate the often rough waters of balancing work, family, and faith. I know that I am good enough because I am loved by you. Show me how to be a woman after your heart who supports and encourages other women to be their true selves too.

Week 9

Creating Balance

Let each person lead the life that the Lord has
assigned to him, and to which God has called him.

1 Corinthians 7:17 ESV

The years I was raising my kids and working full-time were some of the most challenging years in my life. It was a difficult time to "create" balance. I had a lot of responsibility at work and at home! The best way I've learned to create balance in life is by spending time praying, reading God's Word, and seeking God through an ongoing dialogue with Him. We need His divine guidance to help discover our purpose in life, determine what's important, and set priorities.

Each season of life brings new challenges. It takes a bit of experimenting to discover what we need to keep our balance. However, if we seek God and meditate on the Word, we will find the "righteousness, peace, and joy" that can sustain us through difficult times, with balance and purpose.

Carol Doyel
Editor-in-Chief at *LivingBetter50*

What's Important?

Seek the Lord and his strength;
seek his presence continually!

1 Chronicles 16:11 ESV

*W*ork-life balance is challenging, both to attain and maintain. Yet with careful planning and prioritizing, I believe a state of harmony can be achieved. There were years of heavy travel when I invited a friend or family member to join me for any trips lasting three or more nights. I'd work during the day and we'd enjoy each other's company in the evening.

Make time for what's important or you only short-change yourself. That's why even when I'm on the road, I try to find a Catholic church where I can attend Mass every day. That's how I stay grounded and keep the important things of life first and foremost.

God doesn't want you to burn out. He didn't intend for you to fly through this life, running yourself ragged. While balance may seem unattainable at times, it's something God desires for you, and will help you find, if you seek Him.

Dina Dwyer-Owens
Cochair of The Dwyer Group, Inc.
Appeared on *Undercover Boss*

God's Building Blocks

Take delight in the Lord, and he will
give you the desires of your heart.

Psalm 37:4

" *I* can fix this. I can make it better."
Those words have been ringing in my head (and my heart) for as long as I can remember. Regardless of the circumstances, I had this unrelenting desire to get involved in some way and help "make things better." Even when I tried to take a backseat, something drew me in. I had to make a difference, even in the smallest way.

As I look back, those moments have all been building blocks for God's calling on my life. My mission field just happens to be the workplace. Having the opportunity to impact those from all walks of life and demonstrate God's love and grace has been more than a privilege. My desire to do more only grows as I continue to seek His will. How can you demonstrate God's love and grace to someone today?

Kathy F. Belton
Execution Planning Manager with ExxonMobil
Research & Engineering Company

Being a Woman Is an Advantage

Let your manner of life be worthy
of the gospel of Christ,

Philippians 1:27 ESV

*I*n my experience in the workplace, being a woman is actually advantageous. One, you stand out. Two, many companies recognize the importance of attracting and retaining women to create a more balanced and successful business. This often gives women leverage to step up and ask for things that our mothers and grandmothers may not have had.

But the moment women step out of the office, not much has changed. The opportunities available to women have increased hundred-fold, but the entrenchment of "sides"—at work versus at home—cripples women as a whole, instead of empowering us to ask for more.

As women in the workplace, we have unique opportunities to be a living example of God's grace and strength to those with whom we work. How can you live out your faith today?

Laura Kauer Rodriguez
Managing Director of Bulldog Innovation Group

When to Cut Back

"Be still, and know that I am God; I will be exalted
among the nations, I will be exalted in the earth."

Psalm 46:10

*E*very woman I know experiences pressure to do more,
whether at work, with family, at church, or with countless worthy causes. Cutting back isn't easy, even when you
know you need to. Besides the basic discomfort that comes
along with saying no, there's a deeper issue of value and
self-worth at play. In our do-more culture, we've all learned
to associate busyness with importance and purpose, believing that if we're not always doing "something," we must be
wasting our time.

Consider all the times in the Bible when we're called not
to action but to stillness, to consideration, and to waiting.
By cutting back, you're opening up. You're creating space
to breathe, to grow, and to hear and respond to God's call
on your life. What could be more important than that?

Diane Paddison
Founder of 4word women
Former Executive Team at Trammell Crow Company,
CBRE, and ProLogis

REFLECT & REFRESH

Is there something you need to say no to in order to put God first?

Ask God to show you where you need to cut back or re-prioritize in order to create space to listen to Him.

How can you demonstrate God's love and grace to someone in need today?

Lord, I want to do your will. Help me put you and your Word first so that I can find the "righteousness, peace, and joy" that I know will sustain me when times are tough. Give me the wisdom to know when to say yes and when to say no, pursuing your best for me instead of what the world tells me to do. I want to make space in my life to listen and respond to your voice.

Week 10

Pound the Pavement

You yourselves know how you ought to follow
our example. We were not idle when we were with you,
nor did we eat anyone's food without paying for it.
On the contrary, we worked night and day, laboring and
toiling so that we would not be a burden to any of you.

2 Thessalonians 3:7–8

Thousands of wannabes flood into Hollywood daily to find stardom. Sadly, few do. Success in the entertainment and media industry, as in all areas of life, comes when individuals do the hard work—the foundational work of pounding the pavement.

God wants us to pound the pavement in our spiritual lives. Each day is an opportunity to meet someone, read, or learn something that can make you and those you meet stronger in God's kingdom. God's got plans laid out for you to be His star if you follow Him diligently, keeping your eyes open for those doors He'll open. Now, as we say in Hollywood, "Action!"

Kathleen Cooke
Cofounder of Cooke Pictures and The Influence Lab
4word Advisory Board Member

God's Disruption

Therefore, my brothers and sisters, make every effort to confirm your calling and election. For if you do these things, you will never stumble.

2 Peter 1:10

I had a corporate marketing career and climbed the proverbial ladder as fast as I could. Then God placed the desire on my heart to share the love of Jesus with atheists in my secular workplace in an authentic way that wasn't forceful or offensive. This desire blossomed into my company, Prayer Packages. We're able to deliver something with God's love behind it directly to those in need of prayer, encouragement, and inspiration.

The right move is often something we never thought would be right, or even an option. You will likely encounter many confusing and unclear things that may seem like detours, but if you have bold faith, actively seek God's will, and speak to Him often through prayer, you'll eventually (in God's timing) make the leap of faith He's had planned for you all along.

Tiffany Black
Founder of Prayer Packages

Cry Out

And my God will meet all your needs according
to the riches of his glory in Christ Jesus.

Philippians 4:19

*A*fter my husband passed away, there were so many decisions to make. Who was going to be my security blanket? One day I read 2 Kings 4:1–7, which told about a widow in need. Elisha asked the widow two questions before performing a miracle: "What do you want me to do?" and "What do you have?"

Those questions inspired my newfound mission and plan for action: 1) Identify my need and realize that whenever God takes, He never takes all, 2) Realize God gives hope and help for each unique situation, and 3) Cry out, obey, and watch in faith as God changes, renews, and revitalizes lives.

As I met with lawyers and financial planners, God opened doors of support. Like the widow in the story, I had "little oil," but it became more as I walked by faith. Do you have "a little oil"?

Sheila Bailey
President of Sheila B. Ministries, Inc.

Time for Change?

Our boast is this, the testimony of our conscience, that
we behaved in the world with simplicity and godly sin-
cerity, not by earthly wisdom but by the grace of God.

2 Corinthians 1:12 ESV

*I*t's easy to "give your best" at a job that energizes you.
It's much harder to bring excellence to a job you dis-
like. It's not that your feelings about your job don't matter.
They do. God cares about our struggles, big and small.
But He calls us to obedience. God is honored when we
humble ourselves to work "all out" for Him, regardless of
our circumstances.

Don't sit idly in a job that's leaving a horrible taste in
your mouth. Consider what's going wrong and how you
can remedy your current professional position. The answer
might be a minor correction or a drastic career switch.
Before making any change, spend time with God, making
sure He's the one guiding you.

Diane Paddison
Founder of 4word women
Former Executive Team at Trammell Crow Company,
CBRE, and ProLogis

Not the Time

And we know that in all things God works
for the good of those who love him,
who have been called according to his purpose.

Romans 8:28

*W*hen the announcement was made that my employer was merging with another company, I was filled with concern whether I would lose my new promotion. I soon learned that I could keep my newly promoted position if I relocated to another state. After a sleepless night seeking God's guidance, I decided this was not the right time to relocate.

I wondered (fretted) about whether I had made the right decision. Six months later, my routine visit to a doctor led to the discovery of cancer. If I had moved, a visit to a doctor would have been a low priority, risking my life.

Even though I was not 100 percent certain of my decision and I felt the pain of a lost promotion, I could see then God had been at work. Never doubt His all-knowing guidance.

Kim King
Author of *When Women Give*
Former Chief Attorney of Compliance
at ExxonMobil Corporation

REFLECT & REFRESH

Like Elisha and the widow, ask God, "What do you want me to do?" and prayerfully wait for His response.

Does your job energize you and allow you to use your God-given strengths and passions? If so, praise God for the opportunity He has given you. If not, seek His wisdom for the direction your career should take.

What step can you take today to "pound the pavement" in your spiritual life?

Lord, when I'm unsure of what I should do next, help me trust you to show me the path forward and be willing to take a risk when you prompt me to make a move. When I feel like I have just a "little oil," bring people across my path to support me and offer wisdom and guidance in line with your will. Help me to never doubt your all-knowing guidance and respond with obedience.

Week 11

Guard Your Heart

Guard your heart above all else,
for it determines the course of your life.

Proverbs 4:23 NLT

*B*eing a nanny, like most jobs, has its challenging days, when it's easy to lose sight of my purpose. Why am I here? What do I have to offer? In Philippians 4:7, Paul talks about rejoicing in the Lord, not being anxious, lifting our requests to God, and how the Lord will then grant us peace and guard our hearts.

Guard my heart from what? I believe the enemy attacks us with thoughts of doubt and insignificance. Knowing I can present these unrestful thoughts to God is very comforting. In Philippians 4:8 ESV, Paul tells me to think about whatever is true, honorable, just, pure, lovely, commendable, excellent, and worthy of praise. When I focus on this, the Lord gives me peace and strengthens me to get through the tough days. Guard your heart against the enemy today and delight in where God has placed you.

Kiersten Atkinson
Nanny

You're Being Molded

Commit to the Lord whatever you do,
and he will establish your plans.

Proverbs 16:3

I worked in advertising after college, until my employer downsized. I found myself unemployed for around six months. One day, I saw a posting to drive a school bus. At first, I passed over it. Then I took a closer look. Health benefits, paid holidays, and summer break. I decided it was worth a shot and applied.

Jumping from advertising to bus driver was met with lots of speculation and raised brows from those who knew me. But I felt this was where God wanted me. Was it what I thought I'd be doing? No. But driving that school bus became one of the most rewarding things I've ever done. I became part of dozens of students' lives and which blessed me more than I thought it would.

Don't turn up your nose at your current location in life. Your discomfort or embarrassment is God molding you to His perfect plan.

Jordan Johnstone
Writer and Digital Community Manager for 4word

Have Courage

Be strong and courageous. Do not be afraid or terrified because of them, for the Lord your God goes with you; he will never leave you nor forsake you.

Deuteronomy 31:6

When my teenage son was arrested, it rocked my faithful Christian, professionally successful world. I told my boss what had happened. Then I asked for something crazy: "I need to leave at 2:00 every day to pick my son up from school and be with him at home."

In that moment, I knew I was putting my career on the line. Our conversation could easily have led to my resignation, but it didn't. My boss backed me up. I started working from home part-time and pouring into my son.

You could lose your job tomorrow or feel God calling you to be home with your kids. Have the courage to risk stepping out in faith. God's plans go far beyond your wildest dreams or fears.

Diane Paddison
Founder of 4word women
Former Executive Team at Trammell Crow Company, CBRE, and ProLogis

Peer to All

There is neither Jew nor Gentile, neither slave nor free,
nor is there male and female, for you are all one in
Christ Jesus.

Galatians 3:28

In Paul's day, Jews were considered better than Greeks, free people were perceived as being superior to slaves, and men were valued far above women. Paul says that in God's eyes, we're not loved any more or less because of our gender, ethnicity, or socioeconomic status. One of our jobs as believers is to promote God's kingdom of justice and mercy here on earth.

If we approach our work environment as a peer to all colleagues, we create opportunities for meaningful dialogue. If we act respectfully toward all our coworkers, we convey a portion of God's kindness toward His people.

As women, we can lead conversations that help everyone recognize that we're a stronger business, organization, and society, when we fully utilize the talents of all who are called to a particular field—men or women.

Elizabeth Knox
Author of *Faith Powered Profession*
Founder of MatchPace

Unforgettable Hug

"For I know the plans I have for you," declares the Lord,
"plans to prosper you and not to harm you, plans to
give you hope and a future."

Jeremiah 29:11

I have forgotten a lot of hugs; not that one. I was a bit stunned by the length of the hug from this beautiful, tall, young woman I'd admired and shared a cubicle with, but I knew she was praying for me, blessing me, encouraging me in that silence. I earned this unforgettable hug because I had just been "let go" for the very first time from my very first "professional" job—and I had bought a house the month before.

Jeremiah 29:11 wasn't always on my lips, as it is now. I didn't realize at the time, but my colleague's faith was enough at that moment. It didn't magically make the anxiety about the future go away, but it did show a glimmer of God's hand in what was to come.

Crystal Roznik
Owner of Duck Soap Box Creative

REFLECT & REFRESH

Has a drastic change in life circumstances ever affected your work? How did you see God at work in that season?

What lies do you need to guard your heart against?

Is there a coworker God may be calling you to share His love with? How can you demonstrate God's love at work?

Lord, thank you for blessing me with the opportunity to use the gifts and talents you've given me to contribute in my workplace. Thank you for placing coworkers in my life that I can encourage, uplift, and bless, and thank you for putting women and men in my path to do the same for me. Show me who may need a word of encouragement or a reassuring hug today, and help me be responsive to your call to love and respect those I work with. Above all, help me trust you to guide my career path and bring the right opportunity at the right time.

Week 12

Prayer Labyrinth

And pray in the Spirit on all occasions with all kinds of prayers and requests. With this in mind, be alert and always keep on praying for all the Lord's people.

Ephesians 6:18

I went on an epic journey with a bunch of friends and warrior women. Together, we went back in time. I went back and remembered everything God had invited me to be part of.

As a group, what we did was a prayer labyrinth. It's a huge circle with a meandering path that winds and turns, leading into the center, and then out again. The path is designed for reflection. It's meant to help you clear your mind, yet it was so frustrating.

The long and winding road of prayer can be both frustrating and rewarding. This exercise reminded me that we're all on a journey, all the time, with a lot of amazing people. I'm trying to pay more attention—not to just "get somewhere," but to enjoy the path there.

Danielle Strickland
Salvation Army Officer—Justice Advocate

Only God

"Seek first his kingdom and his righteousness,
and all these things will be given to you as well."

Matthew 6:33

*P*eople ask me, "How did you build a successful company, raise three kids, stay married to the same man and keep him happy in the process?" Only God. "Balance" is a myth. When you put God first, the rest falls into place.

God gave me the wisdom to know that my marriage and children were more important than my business. I set clear boundaries on my time and energy. I disciplined myself to rise early and take time to talk with God to prepare my day. I learned to lead myself, following Jesus' example, and determined my priorities through His words.

If you wish to be successful, adopt Jesus' example and wisdom. Lead yourself with that inspiration. You'll find your path a little straighter and your life much more enriched.

Kathryn M. Tack
Executive Coach of Executive Coach, Inc.
Former CEO of Good Times, a multimillion dollar franchise
in hospitality/management
4word Board Member

Pruning Brings Joy

"He cuts off every branch in me that bears no fruit,
while every branch that does bear fruit he prunes
so that it will be even more fruitful."

John 15:2

I decided to try gardening on my tiny apartment patio. I started with a single succulent and graduated to peppers, strawberries, herbs, sunflowers, and a jasmine vine!

After leaving town for a few days, I came home to a wilted strawberry plant. Distraught, I asked a local expert for advice. "Prune away the fruit and any dead stems," she explained. "Don't try to save the fruit at the expense of the whole plant—the fruit will grow back!"

I cut my strawberry plant down to just two pitiful leaves. To my surprise, what was left of the plant showed immediate improvement.

God doesn't enjoy pruning the wilted areas of our lives. But imagine the infinite and unimaginable joy He feels as He watches us grow and bear fruit.

Lisa Sack
Manager of Operations and Human Resources, 4word

In Love

Instead, speaking the truth in love, we will grow to become
in every respect the mature body of him who is the head,
that is, Christ. From him the whole body, joined and held
together by every supporting ligament, grows and builds
itself up in love, as each part does its work.

Ephesians 4:15–16

*B*eing successful in the workplace requires that we use our strengths and abilities to do work we are passionate about and to which God leads us. I call this the "can do," the "want to," and " the led to" of our lives. I've found this combination to be a good formula for making career decisions.

One of my natural strengths has always been "speaking the truth," which requires both critical thinking skills as well as the courage and boldness to speak up in difficult situations. The "in love" part was, unfortunately, not one of my natural strengths! It often resulted in the painful process of failing, praying, changing, and learning as I grew up in Christ.

As Christians we are called to "speak the truth in love" as we grow and build others up through our work. Which part of "speaking the truth in love" comes most naturally to you, and which part do you need to ask for God's help with as you do your work?

Bonnie Wurzbacher
Chief Resource Development Officer, World Vision International

Get a Spiritual Habit

Devote yourselves to prayer,
being watchful and thankful.

Colossians 4:2

*D*o you strive to develop habits to set yourself up for success? It's also important to develop spiritual habits, like prayer.

Set a time to pray every day. Put it on the calendar, like a meeting for work! Then, come up with a prayer strategy. Decide what and who to pray for and how to monitor results. Consider starting a prayer journal. It's my favorite way to pray. It's so encouraging to look back at my prayers over the years and see how God answered them.

Once you've developed a consistent prayer "habit," think of other spiritual habits you can incorporate into your life. Keep your goals attainable. Spiritual habits shouldn't be a source of stress in your life, but rather a source of joy. Open your heart to what God would have for you to do and know that He will help you see your goals to completion!

Lori Berry, MA-PC
Pastoral Counselor
4word Advisory Board Member

REFLECT & REFRESH

*What can you do today to "pay more attention" and en-
joy the journey the Lord has you on, instead of rushing
to get to the next place?*

*Determine one step you can take today to set clearer
boundaries around your time and energy.*

*Set a time every day to pray, and put it on your calendar.
See what God does through your commitment to seek
Him in prayer!*

Lord, help me seek your balance for my life, putting my faith and family above all else. Show me
what boundaries I need to set up in my life to
protect and nurture those you have placed in my
care, and help me to make setting aside time with
you a priority. If there are things in my life that
need to be pruned away so that I can grow and
bear fruit, help me to cut them away, trusting that
you will bring abundant growth to my life.

Week 13

Don't Fear Feedback

Everyone should be quick to listen,
slow to speak and slow to become angry

James 1:19

*W*e all want to be the type of person who humbly and honorably receives and responds to feedback. But the truth is most of us aren't. *I welcome feedback*, we think, *when it's valid. Or when it comes from someone I respect. Or when it's delivered appropriately.*

Christians are called to seek and meditate on truth, even truth that may be hard to hear. We have the freedom to do that because we don't have to be fearful of or constrained by the feedback the world offers. God offers us an identity in Him that cannot be threatened by employee evaluations or criticism from family members.

The next time you encounter feedback that makes you uncomfortable, offer a quick prayer and realign your heart and mind. Then, secure in your foundation, open yourself to truth and growth.

Diane Paddison
Founder of 4word women
Former Executive Team at Trammell Crow Company,
CBRE, and ProLogis

Pursuit of Excellence

All those the Father gives me will come to me,
and whoever comes to me I will never drive away.

John 6:37

The driving force behind many accomplished women is a spirit and pursuit of excellence. This spirit is what helps us achieve great things, but it can also be our biggest spiritual challenge! Our need to be perfect can also be the thing that creates self-condemnation, a spirit of striving, not resting, and a lack of joy and peace.

The reality is that our identity cannot be in the things we achieve—it must be in Christ.

It's hard to let go of the world's evaluation of who we are and fully embrace the peace, joy, and affirmation that come simply from being a daughter of Christ—nothing more, nothing less. Christ's love is not dependent on my actions and accomplishments. How much freedom could we experience if we actually loved ourselves that same way?

Sheeba Philip
VP of Marketing Strategy & Communications, JCPenney

Your Finest Hour

You, dear children, are from God and have overcome them, because the one who is in you is greater than the one who is in the world.

1 John 4:4

*I*s your work your mission field? Are you prepared to do extraordinary things for God?

Our culture is constantly demeaning God's Word and demanding its way. The tactics of the enemy are to cast doubt and fear over believers, and to create a dark time and culture wars in America. We must stand on God's promises and resist the lies of the culture. Every situation—even when painful or difficult—is an opportunity to know Christ more intimately, and for others to know Christ too.

Are you ready to do extraordinary things with God? He wants to use you for His glory as His tool in your workplace. You can only do something today, and you can only take action now. Today is your finest hour!

Virginia Prodan, Esq.
Author of *Saving My Assassin*

Plant Seeds

Therefore go and make disciples of all nations.

Matthew 28:19

*J*esus commanded all believers to share our faith. The expectation was not to set up institutions and degrees to qualify people to take over the job of sharing faith. Nope. It was—and still is—meant to be everyone's job.

What that looks like is different for each of us. It might mean taking a moment to pray silently before a team lunch. Perhaps it means responding to a stressful or threatening situation with, "Let me take some time to pray about that, and I'll get back to you."

The point is to plant seeds that provide openings and provoke thoughts. Then, if we are invited, we get to talk about our faith and salvation in Jesus. It's really that easy. If we are rejected, we know God could use our conversation to make changes in people's lives decades afterward.

What opportunities will today bring?

Lori Berry, MA-PC
Pastoral Counselor
4word Advisory Board Member

Don't Be Pushy

Let your conversation be always full of grace,
seasoned with salt, so that you may know
how to answer everyone.

Colossians 4:6

*H*ow can we bring our faith into our workplace without being pushy or overbearing? Most of us struggle with finding the right balance. I remember meeting a friend for lunch, who bowed to pray before eating, which I love to do if I'm with someone who shares my faith. However, she was incredibly loud and obvious, like she wanted others to see and hear her.

Paul encourages us to "know how to answer" everyone. In other words, people are watching. In my experience, our actions speak louder than words and give us the platform to "answer."

We need to be smart about where and when we express our faith. It doesn't mean we don't speak up, but it does mean that we pick our battles. Ask God to direct your conversations and your actions. Then be ready to give an answer!

Susan DiMickele
SVP & General Counsel, National Church Residences

REFLECT & REFRESH

Do you believe that "Christ's love is not dependent on my actions and accomplishments"? If not, why?

What does sharing your faith at work—your mission field—look like for you?

What step can you take today to make sure you are "ready to give an answer" to anyone who asks about your faith?

Lord, help me see my work as more than a place I spend forty hours a week to take home a paycheck. Help me understand that you have given me my workplace as a mission field, a place to share you with those I come into contact with each day. Forgive me when I fail to be a light among my coworkers and clients. Teach me to share my faith boldly in an authentic way and to represent you well in all that I do, knowing that because my identity is in you alone, I am free!

Week 14

Moment by Moment

For Christ's sake, I delight in weaknesses, in insults,
in hardships, in persecutions, in difficulties.
For when I am weak, then I am strong.

2 Corinthians 12:10

*S*truggling with Lyme disease has been one of the most humbling experiences of my life. For a time, I was angry with God and grieving the loss of my healthy self. But now I depend on Him, moment by moment. I know He only allows things in my life—including suffering—for my good and the good of others.

I'm no longer independent, but rather *dependent* on my Savior in every way. So many things that mattered to me before are no longer important, like keeping my house immaculate or worrying about my image. What has become increasingly more important is how I can let God's light shine through my life and show that even in my weakness and pain, I can be a beacon of His love, provision, and grace.

Stephanie Thompson-Buttice
Lead Advisor/Relationship Manager at Human Investing

Like a Toddler's Love

Great is your love toward me;
you have delivered me from the depths.

Psalm 86:13

God's love is like that of a young toddler. He runs and hugs us, no matter what we're facing, how our day is going, or how we may have failed.

God's love is both great and personal. In Psalms, David is honest about the wrath he is facing from evil people who mean to do him harm. But he felt God's love in the midst of his trial, proclaiming, "Great is your love toward me." David longed for an undivided heart for God, and he wanted to respond to God's love for him by committing himself totally to God.

When hope starts to elude us, we can turn to the true love that God has for us and trust in His promises. Be encouraged today by God's promises, and never stop hoping and trusting that He will do what He says.

Diane Paddison
Founder of 4word women
Former Executive Team at Trammell Crow Company,
CBRE, and ProLogis

Reasoning with God

"Come now, and let us reason together,"
says the Lord.

Isaiah 1:18 NKJV

One July morning, I watched my husband suffer cardiac arrest. On the emergency call, I began praying. First I bargained with God. When I realized I was bargaining, I shifted to begging, quoting Isaiah 1:18 NKJV, "'Come now, let us reason together,' says the LORD." Reasons my husband's life could not, should not, be over began to pour out of me.

I remember being surprised as words from Isaiah came out of my mouth. I shouldn't have been; I unabashedly love the book of Isaiah. What came out of me were the hours of reading and loving words from Isaiah stored in my memory bank.

One day we'll all face a crisis. Fill up with the goodness of God, His Word, His love, and His past actions of grace in your life. When a crisis comes what fills you will be what flows out of you.

Suzanne Matthews
Author of *Unlocking Belief: Answering Questions Jesus Asks*

Ignoring Red Flags

He said to me, "My grace is sufficient for you,
for my power is made perfect in weakness."
Therefore I will boast all the more gladly about
my weaknesses, so that Christ's power may rest on me.

2 Corinthians 12:9

*O*ne of my most defining lessons in waiting on God's timing came during my years of singleness. In my conservative Christian community, women routinely got married in college. I didn't easily fit into a category at church. I even started going to services late to avoid the looks of pity or the awkward set ups.

Unfortunately, it took me a decade to lose the feeling of insecurity over my singleness. I stopped praying for a man, and instead prayed for contentment with the life God had given me. That is when God blessed me with my sweet husband.

We need to trust that God's plan and timing are sovereign. It is not about our self-sufficiency, because His grace is abundantly sufficient.

Sandra Crawford Williamson
CEO of Crawford Creative Consulting
4word Advisory Board Member

Secret to Moving Forward

When hard pressed, I cried to the Lord;
he brought me into a spacious place.

Psalm 118:5

My secret to moving forward when everything seems to be going against you is to be determined, to know what you want, what you need, what you will not sacrifice, and to have confidence. The *most* important thing is to have faith, patience, peace, and understanding that God knows what's best. He has a plan for you, and He will lead you down it.

If things seem to be falling apart around you, don't panic! I know that's easier said than done, but it makes everything harder on you and your family. Stay poised, determined, and faithful. Do something for yourself every day that will help keep your stress level under control.

God has always had a plan for your life, even when you don't believe Him. Risk trusting that fact. It will provide peace through the hard times.

Noël Borchardt
PMO Director at a healthcare software company
Advanced Director with Pampered Chef

REFLECT & REFRESH

In a world that values independence, do you feel you are dependent on the Lord?

What is one example of a time you felt God's love in the midst of a trial or hardship?

Do you have a group of family or friends who are there to support you when times are tough? If not, what steps can you take to find your "tribe" to walk with you through the hard times?

Lord, I admit that I often strive to be independent, taking care of myself and those around me before seeking your help and your provision. Teach me to be dependent on you so I can know the peace and freedom that comes from laying down my independence and picking up my cross to follow you daily. Thank you for loving me in times of struggle, especially through those you have given me to walk with on the difficult days. Thank you for always providing for me in your perfect love.

Week 15

Seasons of Leaning

In vain you rise early and stay up late,
toiling for food to eat—for he grants sleep
to those he loves.

Psalm 127:2

I've learned that juggling all the roles involved in being a "mamapreneur" is seemingly impossible. I worked endless hours with very little or no sleep. I prayed and prayed and prayed for balance. Ultimately, my body was literally shutting down.

So I took ten days and did NOTHING. I was ordered to not let my brain "turn on" other than to watch mindless movies and TV. It was incredibly hard, but it was the start toward "healthy balance."

I now realize the importance of balance and work toward it daily as a goal. Accept the fact that there will be seasons of "leaning," leaning a little more into business, leaning more into family, etc. Making "balance" a goal is good—but don't beat yourself up if you don't get there. There's even balance in our pursuit of finding balance!

Melissa Hinnant
Owner/Designer of Grace and Lace
Appeared on *Shark Tank*

It's Going to Get Messy

For in the day of trouble
he will keep me safe in his dwelling.

Psalm 27:5

*L*ife will get messy, I promise you. Illnesses are inevitable. Friendships will come and go according to our season of life. You and your significant other will have some real "lows" in your relationship. Time to throw in the towel and find a dark room to sit in? Absolutely not.

In this sinful, imperfect world we live in, mess is going to happen. But I'm learning to view a mess as an opportunity to be positive, resourceful, and learn more about the grace and power of my God. When I let my perfectionist facade fall away, the ability to find peace and rest in whatever situation I'm in truly is an act of God.

The next time a mess enters your life, hold back the urge to freak out. Try to view that beautiful mess for what it is: an opportunity to grow.

Jordan Johnstone
Writer and Digital Community Manager for 4word

Listen to Him

"For where your treasure is,
there your heart will be also."

Luke 12:34

*I*f you don't have priorities, life is just going to roll at you. There are parts of life you should just roll with, but often there's so much coming at you at once that knowing which big pebbles need to be put in the jar first to allow space in your life is a challenge.

Need help with setting priorities? Connect with like-minded women. People who are dying on the vine are people who aren't in community. People set goals for their career, but they don't always set them for their spiritual life or their relationships, so things just start to happen. Sometimes, they don't happen very well. Then all of a sudden, you're living this life that you didn't expect to be living. Having a support system in place will not only help you set your life's priorities and goals, it will help you *keep* them.

Lyn Cook
Senior Community Group Director,
Redeemer Presbyterian Church

"No" Is Crucial

By the seventh day God had finished the work he had been doing; so on the seventh day he rested from all his work.

Genesis 2:2

The word "no" is crucial to effectively stewarding your God-given gifts, and it's a part of God's example. On the seventh day of creation, God rested. Creating was good, and I'm sure God could have continued, but there came a time to say, "No more."

If you're considering something that doesn't fit your strengths or priorities, say no, if possible. I said no to school and activity requests when my children were young. In doing so, I protected my ability to give my best to the work God created me for.

Don't feel guilty for saying no, when it results in you being a faithful steward. God would rather you serve Him in a few areas with maximum effort, than wearily push yourself through numerous obligations.

Diane Paddison
Founder of 4word women
Former Executive Team at Trammell Crow Company, CBRE, and ProLogis

Stop Pretending

I praise you because I am fearfully and wonderfully made; your works are wonderful, I know that full well.

Psalm 139:14

*I*t's hard to walk in confidence when we're constantly comparing ourselves to others. No matter how good we feel or look, how talented we may be, or even how successful we are, there is always going to be someone else who is better. It's easy to get caught up in the comparison game, especially when we're competing for position at work, church, or even in our own home.

When you're so busy comparing yourself to others, you are rejecting God's perfect design for you. You can't be who He created you to be if you're pretending to be someone else. Accepting yourself as His creation lets you become the confident, shining star He intended you to be. May the Lord help us learn to truly appreciate each other's gifts, and enjoy—even treasure—the wonder of being exactly who He created us to be.

Lisa Creed
Owner of Good News Coaching

REFLECT & REFRESH

Are you afraid to "do nothing" for even one day? How could taking a day off help you re-prioritize and find balance?

Set a goal for your spiritual life or relationships this week and commit to achieving it. Consider bringing a friend alongside you for accountability.

Do you struggle with comparing yourself to others? Jot down five things you are grateful for today. Then, ask the Lord to help you appreciate the blessings and gifts of others.

Lord, as I stare at an ever-growing to-do list, help me remember that you haven't asked me to find "balance" in my life—you only ask me to seek you first. Show me the priorities you have for my life, and give me the confidence to say no to anything that doesn't line up. Thank you for the many blessings and gifts you have given me. Kill the root of comparison in my life as I pursue an attitude of gratitude each day.

Week 16

Return the Favor

Preach the word; be prepared in season and
out of season; correct, rebuke and encourage—
with great patience and careful instruction.

2 Timothy 4:2

I was in Shreveport, Louisiana, hoping to find my way to Austin, Texas, when a friend introduced me to Kerri, who became my career coach and mentor. Kerri went above and beyond, helping me clean up my résumé, offering interview tips, and providing pep talks. She connected me with a startup media group in Austin, and after months of interviews I was hired!

First, I credit my success to the Lord. He's blessed me beyond measure. I count Kerri as one of those blessings. She connected me with amazing people doing amazing things that inspire me. Listening and learning from those who've gone before us allows us to avoid unnecessary mistakes and better position ourselves for success.

Women in the workplace, seek out ways to inspire and encourage the next generation. Return the favor of those who changed your life.

Jordan Ring
Ethical Style Director

All Rolled into One

The purposes of a person's heart are deep waters,
but one who has insight draws them out.

Proverbs 20:5

The term *mentor* can carry a lot of weight. We want one person who is a parent, coach, boss, therapist, and best friend—as well as someone who can just hand us a new job—all rolled into one.

In reality, we won't find that all in one person. No single person is going to be able to fill all those roles, and no single mentor is going to be able to help us with the countless situations we're going to encounter as we move through life. Having several people we can go to for advice is actually more beneficial, and more effective, than having a single mentor.

Ask God to show you your mentors. Seek those around you who can come alongside you and be just the right piece to help you put together life's puzzle.

Elizabeth Knox
Author of *Faith Powered Profession*
Founder of MatchPace

Magic Bridge

And let us consider how we may spur one another
on toward love and good deeds, not giving up
meeting together, as some are in the habit of doing,
but encouraging one another.

Hebrews 10:24–25

*T*oo many women approach mentoring thinking that simply securing the "right" mentor is a magic bridge to vibrant faith, career success, and life balance. Mentoring is powerful. It can lead to great things in your faith, relationships, and career. Finding a mentor is a big first step, but it's only a first step. There's a lot more work to do if you want to make the most of your mentoring relationships!

Before you begin a mentorship, ask God for His direction. Your mentor may be someone you never expected to enter your life. This is what makes mentorship "magical," in my book. Seeing God orchestrate connections and relationships is just one small example of His infinite love for us.

Diane Paddison
Founder of 4word women
Former Executive Team at Trammell Crow Company,
CBRE, and ProLogis

Freedom in Mentoring

So humble yourselves under the mighty power of God,
and at the right time he will lift you up in honor.

1 Peter 5:6 NASB

*M*entoring others isn't simply an option to help other women in their careers. It's actually a biblical mandate. We're compelled by the Great Commission (Matthew 28:18–20). Jesus didn't say we should tell people about Him only if we feel like it, on days when we're in a good mood, or when we think we've got life mastered. He simply said, "Go." That verb urges us to talk to people outside of our normal circle.

As a mentor, you will have a lasting impact on your mentee as you help her find freedom in discerning what is truly important, setting reasonable goals, and striving to be the woman God called her to be. The ripple effects of your guidance will be immeasurable.

Lori Berry, MA-PC
Pastoral Counselor
4word Advisory Board Member

Rite of Passage

*"Be strong and courageous, because you will lead
these people to inherit the land I swore
to their ancestors to give them."*

Joshua 1:6

There's a special blessing covering the relationship between mentor and mentee. Developing leaders and transferring the anointing is a biblical model. A great example of a mentor and mentee relationship is Moses and Joshua. Moses, the mentor, shared his wisdom, leadership and expertise, and developed Joshua, his mentee, over forty years.

God has a specific purpose and anointing for each person. Certainly Moses was disappointed he was not allowed to enter the Promised Land. This blessing was reserved for Joshua, his mentee.

New challenges (like Joshua following in Moses' footsteps) can be frightening, but the Lord wants us to be "strong and courageous." Seek the Lord's calling on your life and seek a mentor to share and pray with you along your journey. Together, you can study God's Word and you just might have tons of fun along the way!

Dr. Brooke Jones
Founder & CEO of Stronger than Espresso

REFLECT & REFRESH

Identify one way you can "return the favor" this week and bless someone who has helped you. Then, do it!

Could you use help figuring out one "piece of the puzzle" in your life? Ask God to bring a mentor alongside you to help you in this season.

Is there a younger woman in your workplace you could reach out to and offer wisdom and guidance? Challenge yourself to get together this week and simply listen.

Lord, thank you for the gift of mentorship and the ability to reach up to those who have gone before me and down to those who are coming up behind me. Remind me that I am blessed to be a blessing. Help me be generous with my time and wisdom with younger women who are in need of a mentor. Help me have eyes to see the variety of mentors you have placed in my life and give me the humility to listen and learn from them.

Week 17

Big Steps

In God, whose word I praise—
in God I trust and am not afraid.

Psalm 56:4

*W*hen I started my own business, fear came knocking on my door like never before. It convinced me I wasn't suited for this new venture. There were days when it robbed me of the progress I was making in fulfilling my dreams.

One day I came across how Moses instructed Joshua to "be strong and take courage" in Deuteronomy 31:6. It was then that I decided to face my fears and fight back with praise and thanksgiving. In doing this, God helped me regain the courage I needed to continue.

To what "big step" is God calling you? Maybe it's a new position in your office, a new outreach at church, or a move across the country. Refuse to allow your trepidation to rob you of the potential joy God has waiting for you. Step out in faith and sing His praises on your journey.

Corine Sandifer
Owner Brentwood Life Coach
Host of Rising Stories Podcast

Painful Journeys

> You know that the testing of your faith produces perseverance. Let perseverance finish its work so that you may be mature and complete, not lacking anything.
>
> *James 1:3-4*

*A*s a pastor's daughter, I was raised in the church with a roadmap described as "biblical" that defined God's purposes for me as a woman. It centered on marriage, home, and family.

By young adulthood, it was clear my life wasn't following that map. This compelled me to go back to Scripture with new questions.

Parts of my journey have been painfully difficult. Yet those hard places challenged me to wrestle with questions I otherwise never would have asked. I've learned God expects a lot of me and all of His daughters; that His vision for us is expansive and wildly creative; that He frees and empowers us to engage the challenges, opportunities, and changes we encounter.

Carolyn Custis James
Author of *Half the Church: Recapturing God's Global Vision for Women* and *The Gospel of Ruth: Loving God Enough to Break the Rules*
4word Advisory Board Member

Self-Assess

"Come to me, all you who are weary and burdened,
and I will give you rest."

Matthew 11:28

*F*eeling stressed? Uncertain? When I start feeling those knots in my stomach, God's Word is the first place I turn. Has my time with God been absent, rushed, or perfunctory? Sometimes the demands of my life—caring for my daughter, running a nonprofit, keeping up with other commitments—are so pressing they pull my focus away from God. These demands are real. They require energy and attention. But it's a mistake to confuse urgency with primacy.

Whether you're bearing heavy burdens or are yoked to Jesus, there are weights to carry either way. What Jesus offers us is Himself. "Don't struggle alone," He says. "Join with me, learn from me, strain with me."

I'm working at my best when I'm with God, bolstered by His purpose. If God is with you, you can conquer today with your "best" too.

Diane Paddison
Founder of 4word women
Former Executive Team at Trammell Crow Company,
CBRE, and ProLogis

Fear Descending

*Whoever dwells in the shelter of the Most High
will rest in the shadow of the Almighty.*

Psalm 91:1

*I*t was a hotel in a major city. We'd stayed there before,
but ignored small indicators of change. A limo idled
near a side entrance. Guests paid in cash at registration. We
were asked to sign a "no partying" form. For a middle-aged
group of clergy, this seemed odd, but not ominous.

Between 2:00 and 4:00 a.m., there were constant footsteps in the hall. When knocking on our door became
persistent—in spite of my husband shouting, "Wrong
room!"—fear gripped me in a new way. I hoped to only be
robbed.

I began to pray Scripture I had not read for months.
Praise God, He spoke through Psalm 91 as I repeated its
words over and over. "You will not fear the terror of the
night . . ." When morning came, we left unharmed.

When fear descends, run and cling to your Father and
His words.

Carol Seiler
Commissioner of The Salvation Army

Defining Moment

I waited patiently for the Lord;
he turned to me and heard my cry.

Psalm 40:1

The phone rang in the middle of the night. I sped to the hospital, where I was able to say goodbye to my father before a second heart attack ended his life. Three months later, my distraught mother committed suicide. I was twenty years old.

My brother is a manic-depressive; my sister suffers from chronic depression. My mother's death threatened to sink me into a pit of fatalism. Was it just a matter of time before I became like them? Our family history of mental illness frightened me.

I wanted a different path. I cried out to God. This became a defining moment. God heard me, rescued me, and provided opportunities to publicly share my story with hurting people. Instead of hiding in shame and embarrassment, I spoke out. As a result, people were healed. And so was I.

Kathryn M. Tack
Executive Coach of Executive Coach, Inc.
Former CEO of Good Times, a multimillion dollar franchise in hospitality/management
4word Board Member

REFLECT & REFRESH

What has your time with God looked like lately? Ask Him to help you carve out time spent just with Him.

Are there circumstances in your life that make you feel afraid? Whether it's a challenge at work, a health scare, or a tense relationship, try praying Scripture, like Joshua 1:6-9 or Isaiah 41:13.

What "big step" is God calling you to take? Pray for the courage to take it.

Lord, I know you don't want me to live in fear of what may come. Thank you for giving me your Word that tells me you are always with me. Take any fear I carry today and replace it with confidence in your plan and protection over my life. When you ask me to take a bold step, give me the courage to take it. Please bring people alongside me to support and encourage me. Help me see the next "big step" you're calling me to take and walk forward in the confidence that you're always with me!

Week 18

No Control

We know that in all things God works
for the good of those who love him, who have
been called according to his purpose.

Romans 8:28

*H*ow many times have we hoped and prayed for something so badly we could actually see it play out in our minds? But we have no control over the outcome. And some things are just not meant to be.

As I think back over the countless times I was waiting for "that moment," regardless of what that moment was, I'm grateful for the times God gently closed that door. At first, I may have been disappointed or even embarrassed. Then I remembered my mother's words: "God doesn't make mistakes. It wasn't meant to be." My mother continued on with whatever she was doing. Simple as that. She wasn't being insensitive, just speaking the truth from her heart. For that, I'm truly grateful, because I learned from her how to accept God's timing and His ways.

Kathy F. Belton
Execution Planning Manager with ExxonMobil
Research & Engineering Company

Feel Like a Misfit?

You have searched me, Lord, and you know me.

Psalm 139:1

*D*o you ever feel like you don't quite fit in with some of the images you see of polished, professional women? Time and again, I've seen women discover they're not the misfit they thought they were, through mentoring. When we connect with a mentor with similar goals, life circumstances, or challenges, we realize we aren't alone. The feeling of being understood can be one of the most empowering experiences in our careers and in our lives.

It took some unlikely mentors in my life to draw out God's purposes for me and give me the confidence to pursue His will in my life. God-sized dreams can feel overwhelming. When we compare ourselves to others, we can feel discouraged from pursuing those dreams. But walking with a mentor can empower us to pursue the God-given purposes in our lives.

Diane Paddison
Founder of 4word women
Former Executive Team at Trammell Crow Company,
CBRE, and ProLogis

Competing Voices

Moses answered them, "Wait until I find out
what the Lord commands concerning you."

Numbers 9:8

God's voice spoke the world into existence and His voice still speaks to us today. However, our lives are filled with competing voices that create noise and can drown out God's voice. To hear God's voice, be relentless in seeking quiet and solitude. The quiet softens the distractions and helps you focus more clearly on the Creator who loves and adores you.

Go to God's Word first, so it can work in harmony and rhythm with the circumstances of everyday life. God's Word reminds us of our true identity, which is not based on what we do, who we know, and what we have, but on how we are uniquely created. Learn to embrace *you*.

As you learn to invite quiet into your life, you will find yourself able to pass your knowledge onto others. Become a poster child for stillness and help others hear His voice.

Debbie Eaton
Mentor, Writer, Leader of influence and change

Not Qualified

A final word: Be strong in the Lord
and in his mighty power.

Ephesians 6:10 NLT

*I*n 2012, God broke my heart for victims of sex trafficking and called me to start a nonprofit organization. I was neither "qualified" nor "equipped" in regards to my own strength, experience, or title.

Over the past several years, I've learned that God is in control of the godless (2 Chronicles 20:6). I've learned that when God opens a door, no person can shut it (Revelation 3:7–8). I've learned that if God builds something, He will sustain it (Psalm 127:1).

I've never understood the fullness of God's grace until now. By grace, God accomplishes His plans through us—we only have to be obedient and allow Him to take the lead. By grace, our weaknesses make room for God's power to be revealed. And by grace, when God calls you He equips you!

Annie Perkins
Cofounder/Board Chairman of Unlock Freedom
Author of *Pure & Simple: A Teenager's Guide to Going Deeper with God*

Keep Walking

For we walk by faith, not by sight.

2 Corinthians 5:7 NKJV

*Y*ou are always with me. You created me. You know me. You LOVE me. You love the good and the bad that make me "me." You are in, and care about, every detail. You know the plans you have for me and you cannot wait to see them happen. You delight in me. You've given me gifts like no other person on earth. You've given me a purpose that is unique. My purpose is not only for others, but it is for *me.* You want me to be content and fulfilled, full of love and compassion. You have things for me to do, but more importantly, people for me to love.

God, I am so overwhelmed with how you love me. Even when I see nothing but obstacles in front of me, you show me glimpses of the beauty on the other side and gently whisper, "Keep walking. Keep walking."

Lori Berry, MA-PC
Pastoral Counselor
4word Advisory Board Member

REFLECT & REFRESH

Has God ever closed a door on something you desperately wanted? How did you see Him work in your life through what you thought was a missed opportunity?

What voices do you need to drown out in your life in order to hear God better?

Is God calling you to something that you feel neither "qualified" nor "equipped" for? Ask Him to give you courage to pursue His plan for your life.

Lord, thank you for the dreams you have given me for my life. Take away any plans I have that do not align with your will, giving me courage to pursue your plan for me. Help me see closed doors not as missed opportunities, but as your direction for my life as you lead me to the very best you have for me. When I don't feel qualified, remind me that I can do all things through you who gives me strength (Philippians 4:13). I am overwhelmed by your love for me!

Week 19

Anger in the Workplace

In your anger do not sin: Do not let
the sun go down while you are still angry.

Ephesians 4:26

*A*s believers, we may try to avoid anger, thinking of it as a selfish and destructive emotion. But Jesus' own anger when He saw the money changers taking advantage of people at the temple, shows us that frustration and anger are not wrong.

Frustration and anger over an injustice at work should inspire us to godly action. Just as Jesus' anger, emotions and all, was held in check by God's Word, so too should our response always be to do the will of God and treat others the way we'd like to be treated.

Anger in itself is not wrong, and frustrations at work need to be dealt with through the lens of God's Word, resolved quickly, and not allowed to grow into a seed of bitterness.

Diane Paddison
Founder of 4word women
Former Executive Team at Trammell Crow Company,
CBRE, and ProLogis

Battle with Negativity

Those who are kind benefit themselves,
but the cruel bring ruin on themselves.

Proverbs 11:17

*A*s Christians, we want to show others the love and kindness of Jesus. Yet, we're often blind to how much unkindness we show others through our negativity.

For me, my kindness blindness was exasperation. Without saying a word, I was often unkind when I communicated negativity through exasperation with my kids, my colleagues, and my husband. When I finally began trying to withhold my negativity, the Holy Spirit allowed me to see just how negative I'd become.

If you're discovering that you battle with negativity, it's not a death sentence! There are steps you can take to bring more positivity to your life, as well as to the lives of those around you. The first step is to confess your struggle to God and ask Him to bring you opportunities to practice being kind. Invite kindness in and watch your life flourish.

Shaunti Feldhahn
Social Researcher
Best-selling Author of *For Women Only*
and *The Kindness Challenge*

Trusting in the Hallway

Consider it pure joy, my brothers and sisters,
whenever you face trials of many kinds.

James 1:2

For the first time in my life, I was quitting one job without having another job waiting. My personal values conflicted with those of my employer, so I decided to leave.

I once heard a pastor ask, "Can you trust God in the hallway, the place where one door has closed and the other hasn't opened?" As I stood in the hallway of my situation, I began to doubt what God was doing and wondered if I'd made the right decision.

Two weeks later, a recruiter asked to submit my résumé to a client hiring for a new position. A few weeks later, I was offered the position! It provided a significant salary increase, benefits—and I shared the same beliefs as my employer. I truly believe God rewarded me for standing strong in my beliefs. Stand strong in your hallway and allow God to work in His time.

Stacy Robinson
Accountant for Zebco Brands, Tulsa, OK

Be Mindful

*Whatever is true, whatever is noble, whatever is right,
whatever is pure, whatever is lovely, whatever is
admirable—if anything is excellent or praiseworthy—
think about such things.*

Philippians 4:8

*P*aul sure knows how to rain down conviction. I read these verses and consider how often my thoughts are more like, "For the love, if I have to tell her one more time . . ."

My thoughts easily become laser-focused on the frustrations of life. Philippians 4:8 is especially interesting in light of recent research on the brain. I'm sure you've heard hippie-sounding quotes like, "What you think about, you become." Well, it turns out the brain does work this way; each thought teaches your brain something.

God is the Great Architect. He's given us brains with incredible plasticity. He knows that if we focus on whatever is true, noble, right, pure, lovely, admirable, excellent, and worthy of praise, those qualities will dwell in us.

Sandra Crawford Williamson
CEO of Crawford Creative Consulting
4word Advisory Board Member

Interrupting Our Plans

"As the heavens are higher than the earth,
so are my ways higher than your ways and
my thoughts than your thoughts."

Isaiah 55:9

*A*fter twenty-five years of comfortable living in the same city, with great jobs, a great church, and great friends, God made it apparent that it was time to move! My teenage son was starting to make bad decisions. He knew his decisions were wrong, but told my husband and me that sometimes kids behave like someone they're not, just to fit in. It was clear God was calling us to give him an opportunity to be the kid God wanted him to be.

Three years and a thousand miles later, I can honestly say that giving him this opportunity was the best decision we ever made. He's now a college freshman, with incredible high school friends and experiences. While change wasn't easy, it taught us that trusting God is a nonnegotiable prerequisite for living supernaturally in the kingdom!

Pam Johnson
Global Business Director at Nike, Inc.
4word Board Member

REFLECT & REFRESH

Do you feel frustrated or angry at work? What is one step you can take to resolve those frustrations in a godly way this week?

Who can you bless with kindness this week?

Are you living in the "hallway" between a closed door and an open one? Ask God to give you patience as you trust Him to open the next door.

Lord, my workplace is often filled with frustration and negativity. Thank you for placing me in my specific job at this time in order to be your light in the darkness. Show me who you want me to extend special care and kindness to today, because you know what is in the heart of each person. Kill any root of negativity in my life so I can be the best example of your hope and love to those you have placed in my path. And when I feel stuck in the "hallway" between opportunities, help me to trust you to show me the next step in your perfect timing.

Week 20

Liberate Yourself

Put on the new self, created to be like God
in true righteousness and holiness.

Ephesians 4:24

*E*ven though I had wonderful, affirming parents, I grew up very insecure. I was the geek, the dork, the nerd, the object of every tease, taunt, and ridicule of my school. And I carried that self-perception all the way into adulthood—even as I became a successful actress.

Many years later, after I came to Christ, He began to heal that little girl inside me that still felt like she had no value or worth. Our culture bombards us with images women feel they have to live up to. But God tells us that really living is to know Him, draw close to Him, and find our identity in Him. When we finally realize that we already have everything we strive so hard to acquire, it's such a liberating revelation.

Nancy Stafford
Actress and Speaker
Author of *Beauty by the Book: Seeing Yourself as God Sees You*

Don't Segregate Your Life

For the Lord will be at your side
and will keep your foot from being snared.

Proverbs 3:26

*D*o you feel confident and capable at work, but overwhelmed and overstretched at home? At work, we solve problems and plan strategically. When unexpected situations arise, we handle them. But step out of the office and so many of the smart, capable, powerhouse workingwomen I know feel utterly inept, overwhelmed, overstretched, and often underutilized.

Too often we try to segregate our lives into different sections, keeping our "business side" away from our "family side" and our "church side." But God is just as present and just as instrumental in developing those business smarts of yours as He has been in developing the rest of your life. It's time to start using all the tools He's given you to lead the very best life you can.

Diane Paddison
Founder of 4word women
Former Executive Team at Trammell Crow Company,
CBRE, and ProLogis

Get Out of Your Own Way

So God created mankind in his own image, in the image
of God he created them; male and female he created
them.

Genesis 1:27

*L*iving from your True Self is not a plan you need to
construct through self-improvement. It is the Genesis
1 message of getting comfortable with the truth that you
were created, just as you are, in God's image.

For Christians, a lot of our faith is self-sacrificing behavior. That's why it feels selfish to us as believers to focus
on ourselves. I get it! But I think that being our True Self
frees us to be less self-focused. When I give a "true self"
answer instead of a managed answer, everyone relaxes and
the atmosphere in the room becomes more genuine and
purposeful. If you are your True Self, you get out of the
way of yourself and allow God to help you be the woman
He created you to be.

Lesa Engelthaler
Senior Associate of Victory Search Group

Contribute to the Greater Good

Each of you should use whatever gift you
have received to serve others, as faithful stewards
of God's grace in its various forms.

1 Peter 4:10

I believe the Lord created us all in very unique ways. We have our natural personalities and tendencies. We also have interests and passions that form as the result of our different life experiences. While learning about ourselves is incredibly important, I encourage you not to stop there.

Once you discover and embrace your strengths and talents, look outward. Ask yourself, "How can my gifts serve others? How can I contribute to the greater good? In what ways can I strengthen the kingdom of God?"

As we learn more about how we were specifically designed and how to best use our gifts, let's remember to keep an outward mind-set. We weren't meant to keep our riches to ourselves, but to pour them out for something bigger. It is in this outpouring that we are fulfilled.

Julie Champion
Founder of Know You Project

You Know Whose You Are

> "Before I formed you in the womb I knew you,
> before you were born I set you apart;
> I appointed you as a prophet to the nations."
>
> *Jeremiah 1:5*

When you know whose you are, you know who you are. This will make it clear what path you're on at home, work, and in relationship to others. The world we live in today, the media, and especially social media, seek to strip us of identity. We're left trying to find value and worth in the approval of people who don't know us at all. This creates loneliness like never before.

I've worked in secular media for many years and often saw this loneliness with famous people and celebrities. But today "regular" people I know experience this all the time. Success can be found, increased, and shared when you walk in the power of your real identity. Jesus knew who He was and why He came. He wants the same for us.

Cynthia Garrett
TV Host, Author, Motivational Speaker, Evangelist

REFLECT & REFRESH

What is your "defense mechanism"? Ask God to help you find your identity and worth in Him alone.

What unique gifts and talents has God given you? Determine one way you can bless others with those gifts this week.

Do you struggle with comparing yourself to images you see in the media and on social media? Take a break from social media for a day and ask God to use that time to renew your mind.

Lord, give me wisdom to see through the lies the world tells me about who I should be, what I should look like, and how I should spend my time. Help me let go of the images of perfection that fill my social media feeds and find my worth in you alone. You created me unlike anyone else, with unique gifts and talents. Remind me that the only opinion that matters is yours. Help me be comfortable being "me." Give me the strength to dream the dreams you have for me, not the dreams the world tells me I should have.

Week 21

God's Intense Love

Jesus Christ is the same yesterday
and today and forever.

Hebrews 13:8

A young staffer in the Presidential Advance office, I arrived at work at 8:00 a.m. An hour later, Secret Service told me to run for my life. Fighting fear and terror as I ran from the White House on September 11, 2001, Hebrews 13:8 came to my mind. I fought the urge to return home to California, because I felt I was in my position "for such a time as this" (Esther 4:14).

The same God who delivered the Israelites through the Red Sea, and the same God who gave His Son as a loving sacrifice, is the same God who knows and deeply cares for each of us, loving us intimately and intensely. He desires for us to come into His ultimate plan and purpose for our lives. He is trustworthy and remains the same yesterday, today, and forever.

Charity Wallace
Founder & Principal of Wallace Global Impact
Senior Advisor at the George W. Bush Institute
4word Advisory Board Member

Waiting Is a Gift

I wait for the Lord, my whole being waits,
and in his word I put my hope.

Psalm 130:5

We all wait. Waiting for "the one," waiting to have children, waiting for a long and overdue promotion at work ... Waiting is a part of life. For the Christian, it is a kingdom imperative that we all experience. There is little we can control in the waiting, but we can be mindful of how we use our words as we wait.

As we wait, we can either align our words with God's or with our destructive feelings. We can carefully weigh our words to speak life, or we can speak death, making the wait even more weighty. In Christ, the waiting offers a gift: a chance to align our minds and hearts with the grace and love available to us in God's Word. In God's Word, our hope is found

Brenda Bertrand
Speaker and Career Clarity Coach
4word Advisory Board Member

Be Open to God

But God is my King from long ago;
he brings salvation on the earth.

Psalm 74:12

*I*n times when we don't understand what God is doing, we're to remain open to Him. Jesus told His disciples to heal the sick, raise the dead, and preach the gospel. In Acts 9:32–42, Peter did just that. In verse 34, a man was healed and jumped right out of bed. God, however, doesn't heal everyone. Why not? It's a mystery.

It's often difficult for me to understand why the Lord has not yet healed my daughter, Annie, from her debilitating years' long battle with chronic pain. What I do know is that in the midst of Annie's painful journey, He is our sovereign God. He is there with us through all suffering and has a plan and purpose. All He requires is we stay open to that plan and those purposes.

Diane Paddison
Founder of 4word women
Former Executive Team at Trammell Crow Company,
CBRE, and ProLogis

Keep Going

I know your deeds,
your hard work and your perseverance.

Revelation 2:2

I've learned that we often have to persevere in the face of trials and challenges so we can grow into what God has for us in the next season. One morning, when I found myself at my wit's end after moving three states away with our newborn daughter, I heard God whisper: "Keep persevering." Bleary-eyed from another night of little sleep and unsure of what the day would hold, I found myself grateful that God would continue to grow my faith and mold me into His likeness as He teaches me to persevere.

Maybe you recently lost your job. Maybe you didn't get that promotion. Maybe a loved one is dealing with a serious illness and you're unsure what you can do. When it seems like one door after another is closing, or bumps and turns keep showing up on the road ahead, seek God. Ask Him for the strength to keep persevering.

Caitie Butler
4word Church Connect Program Manager

Love Yourself

"Love your neighbor as yourself."

Mark 12:31

*C*ontentment is directly related to loving ourself, loving others, and loving God. I came to this realization after I realized the commandment to "love our neighbor" also requires us to love ourselves.

We all know amazing women who demonstrate their love of neighbors by volunteering, taking care of others' needs, and making themselves available to serve. However, we also know women who overcommit, put their friends and families before their own needs, and are pretty harsh on themselves.

I was an "overcommitter." I wasn't showing myself the same care and love I showed others. The voice inside my head was often unloving, extremely self-judging, and downright mean. Once I was aware of this voice, I began to counter it with loving phrases. As the negative voice subsided, so did my discontentment.

How have you shown yourself love lately? If you haven't, pause what you're doing and give yourself the appreciation you need, in order to love others like God asks.

Jennifer Spaulding
Leadership Coach

REFLECT & REFRESH

What are you waiting for today? Ask God to align your heart and mind with His Word as you wait on Him.

Do you believe Jesus is the same yesterday, today, and forever? How would believing this truth help you persevere?

What is one thing you can do to show yourself love this week?

Lord, you know what hard things I am facing today. While I often feel like I have no control over what the day may hold, your Word tells me you are the same today as you were yesterday, and that you will never change. Thank you for the hope that truth gives me. Help me persevere through the trials I face today, and show me how I can love myself as I also seek to love others and you.

Week 22

Don't Squander!

"Let your light shine before others, that they may see
your good deeds and glorify your Father in heaven."

Matthew 5:16

*A*s a leader, I've had the privilege of guiding a team. Part
of that role involves the special opportunity to bring
light to those around me.

It brings me immense joy to watch someone's face light
up when I greet them with a big smile or compliment them
on a job well done. Think back to some of your proudest
moments. Many of them likely involve someone in a leadership role shining the light of positivity and affirmation
into your world.

Leaders, strive to be the light in someone's life, every
day. Don't let one day of opportunity pass without reaching out to a team member or colleague and passing on the
light of God's love. For some, you may be the first and only
source of kindness they encounter that day. Don't squander that precious opportunity!

Dina Dwyer-Owens
Cochair of The Dwyer Group, Inc.
Appeared on *Undercover Boss*

Breathe Fresh Air

You will shine among them like stars in the sky
as you hold firmly to the word of life.

Philippians 2:15

*I*t's amazing to think that in many workplace settings my faith walk with Christ is "a breath of fresh air." The root of this fresh air is the life-giving breath of the Holy Spirit, which breathes into my soul the hope of Christ. I breathe in the presence of God the Spirit. Then I breathe out the message of God as Savior Jesus.

Sometimes the settings where I share that message are painful and contentious, where I serve those discarded by society. Addicts, those infected with HIV/AIDS, and battered women or children have been in my "workplace" of Salvation Army ministry. Christians should share the possibility of "good living" (holiness) and the "living God" (salvation). Daily I want to breathe deeply and carry God's light-giving message into the night. To whom can you breathe fresh air today?

Carol Seiler
Commissioner of The Salvation Army

Live Free

Live as free people, but do not use your freedom
as a cover-up for evil; live as God's slaves.

1 Peter 2:16

*A*s a woman in the workplace, God has called you to work and given you the gifts and the drive you need to succeed. But He called you there and gifted you in those ways in order to do *His work*. Don't worry: you don't have to shout the gospel from atop your desk chair. Simply strive to demonstrate Christ's loving service to the people around you, whether you're their employee or boss.

Shining God's light in the workplace should not be an uncomfortable thing for you or those around you. If you're living solidly in God's will for your life and trusting Him to guide your steps, you'll inherently be a beacon for Him. Your demeanor and actions will be tinged with His love, which in turn will spread joy to those around you.

Diane Paddison
Founder of 4word women
Former Executive Team at Trammell Crow Company,
CBRE, and ProLogis

Give Back

See to it that no one takes you captive through
hollow and deceptive philosophy, which depends
on human tradition and the elemental spiritual forces
of this world rather than on Christ.

Colossians 2:8

*A*s Christians, we're blessed to have the supreme role model in Christ. But we can also learn from the example of leaders God places in our lives.

I was blessed in my first job to have a manager who was known for his intelligence and business success, as well as being a visionary, a teacher, and a coach who left a legacy of kindness and compassion. He taught me many things about leadership. Now it's my time to pass on those lessons.

In my career, I always seek out leaders I can learn from, whether coworkers, bosses, speakers, or industry experts. In turn, I want to "give back" what has been given to me, to be available to coach and mentor in whatever way God calls me.

Pam Johnson
Global Business Director at Nike, Inc.
4word Board Member

Entering a Different Culture

"I have made you a light for the Gentiles,
that you may bring salvation to the ends of the earth."

Acts 13:47

When you enter a different culture, you know perceptions and expectations will differ from your own. The same is true for women in any male-dominated workplace.

In my research, I found most men share a common set of expectations and perceptions that differ from women's. One man I interviewed, a global president of a Fortune 50 company, gave this advice to strong, talented women: Know your audience. Women instinctively know how other women will perceive something, but they don't know how men will.

It's a new skill set for women to learn, but adopting this mind-set will not only have ramifications in our professional life but our spiritual life. What better way to be a light for God in our workplace than to be viewed as a perceptive and understanding colleague?

Shaunti Feldhahn
Social Researcher
Best-selling Author of *For Women Only*
and *For Women Only in the Workplace*

REFLECT & REFRESH

Do you see your workplace as your mission field?

Do you strive to be perceptive and understanding at work? What is one step you can take today to try to understand your coworkers better?

Who can you show God's love to today through a compliment or an act of kindness?

Lord, thank you for giving me a unique mission field in the form of my workplace. Help me understand how to show my coworkers your love instead of shoving the gospel down their throats. Help me live out the fruits of the Spirit, especially peace, patience, and kindness at work, bringing a breath of fresh air to my workplace. Show me who especially needs to experience your love each day and give me opportunities to offer a kind word or be a listening ear to my coworkers.

Week 23

Turn Off

Then, because so many people were coming
and going that they did not even have a chance to eat,
he said to them, "Come with me by yourselves
to a quiet place and get some rest."

Mark 6:31

I've always struggled with turning work off and resting properly, but it's become even harder when caring for a sick daughter and working primarily out of my home office. I know I need rest. It nourishes my health and well-being. Most importantly, it's part of God's design for His people. The first biblical example of this is God's day of rest after Creation. That pattern of work and rest is repeated throughout Jesus' ministry. Jesus saw the value of rest and prioritized it.

If you can't remember the last time you *really* rested, today needs to be the day that changes. We will serve God, others, and ourselves much better if we have been replenished.

Diane Paddison
Founder of 4word women
Former Executive Team at Trammell Crow Company,
CBRE, and ProLogis

Our Master Plan

Unless the Lord builds the house, those who build it labor in vain. Unless the Lord watches over the city, the watchman stays awake in vain.

Psalm 127:1

I woke suddenly—heart racing, mind reeling. Panic attack. Going through a job transition was much more of a spiritual experience than I could ever have imagined. My mind wanted to rush on to the next thing—exhausting myself and my network day and night—to figure out the next step in my career path. But God called me to rest. He spoke Psalm 127 into my heart, reminding me that only when I look to Him and walk in His ways, will He guide my steps and make my work fruitful.

Trusting God for rest when I felt that I needed to work seemed counterintuitive, but God says that He will supply every need when we are called according to His service—and that is not just when we are toiling away.

Alyssa Huber
Marketing Consultant and Founder of Before the Birds

What Are You Neglecting?

But Jesus often withdrew to lonely places and prayed.

Luke 5:16

"*B*utijust" Syndrome is a term I coined to label the excuses we women have for not taking care of ourselves. ("I'm tired, Butijust have one more thing to do.") We're so busy taking care of our teams at work, our families, and everyone else who needs us, we neglect taking time for ourselves.

If you're a "Butijust" sufferer, I have three potential cures for you. First, obey God's design for Sabbath rest. Get work done ahead of time in order to have a chunk of time to rest and recharge. Second, worship regularly. Missing out on corporate worship is missing out on the blessings God has in store for us. Finally, plan (and go on) a spiritual retreat. God waits for us to quiet ourselves so He can speak into our hearts. Let your Father tend to you while you pour out your heart and reflect on His Word. No more "Butijust" Syndrome!

Lori Berry, MA-PC
Pastoral Counselor
4word Advisory Board Member

Take a Sabbath Moment

Very early in the morning, while it was still dark,
Jesus got up, left the house and went off to a solitary
place, where he prayed. Simon and his companions
went to look for him, and when they found him,
they exclaimed: "Everyone is looking for you!"

Mark 1:35–37

*D*o you ever feel guilty for breaking away for a moment
of solitude and peace? Jesus took "Sabbath moments"
many times throughout His life. He didn't worry about
who would be looking for Him, or how His time could
be better spent as the Savior of all of humanity. He recognized the importance of being in solitude with the Lord,
and never apologized for it.

If the one and only Son of God can break away, so can
you. Give yourself permission to take a Sabbath moment—
whether it's a single breath or an entire day. Lavish in this
time with the Lord, and know it was time well spent!

Lisa Sack
Manager of Operations and Human Resources, 4word

God Is with You

"Have I not commanded you?
Be strong and courageous. Do not be afraid;
do not be discouraged, for the Lord your God
will be with you wherever you go."

Joshua 1:9

There have been days when I've been plagued with anxiety, typically related to a health scare involving a loved one when I feel helpless. At work, I was used to being in charge and leading my teams through difficult challenges with solid plans and prepared contingency plans. But even then, the truth is we're actually not completely in charge, nor in control.

When I am most anxious, taking constructive actions and doing what I can to help is only the starting point. It is only by humbly going into God's peace and loving presence that I find true comfort, and I can finally let go and "let God." My prayer is that, moment to moment, I would be aware of God's presence in my life within me and around me.

Marissa Peterson
Former COO of Sun Microsystems
Former 4word Advisory Board Member

REFLECT & REFRESH

When is the last time you truly rested? Ask God to help you create a "rest routine," so you don't get burned out.

Do you suffer from "Butijust" Syndrome? Commit to taking even five minutes each day to set aside life's demands and spend time with God.

What is making you anxious today? Try giving your anxieties to God first before trying to fix each problem yourself.

Lord, I admit that I sometimes let fear and anxiety rule in my heart instead of your love and peace. Instead of resting in you, I constantly strive to fix problems myself. Just as you set aside a day to rest from your creation, help me carve out moments in my day to stop and rest in you. Help me "seek, accept, and surrender" the need to be in control as I cast all my fears on you. You are the one who is in control.

Week 24

Use Your Past

I will speak of your statutes before kings and will not be
put to shame.

Psalm 119:46

Sharing the story of conquering my alcohol addiction
hasn't been easy. I'm a deeply private person, so when
God asked me to share this testimony publicly, I stomped
my foot like a little child, completely unable to fully grasp
what glorious intentions He had in store. I fought with
Him for two weeks, crying every night, because I couldn't
find the strength to put myself out there like that.

Every day I fought Him, my strength and courage grew,
until I finally went public with the victory. What surprised
me has been the reaction of those who share my story! I've
had people reach out to me to offer support, encouragement, and to share in the victory.

If God is nudging you to tell your story, listen! Your
momentary discomfort and embarrassment could result in
countless lives being changed forever. Let God use your
past to shape someone else's future.

Martha Lumatete
Director of Software Procurement

When Plates Fall and Break

Carry each other's burdens,
and in this way you will fulfill the law of Christ.

Galatians 6:2

I should be able to list "Professional Plate Spinner" on my résumé. It can be an impressive balancing act, until the plates crash to the floor. I'm here to say, "It's not the end of the world!"

Here are a few ways to make plate spinning easier: 1) Find other moms like you and proactively support each other; 2) Stop trying to be Wonder Woman and ask for help; 3) Organize your schedule, color-coding categories, and send your spouse/helpers "meeting requests," because when you don't trust your organizational system, your mind stays on high alert, fearful you'll forget something; 4) Carefully select what you can do and be *fully present*; 5) Let go of your guilt.

So when the plates fall and break, put that hot mess back together and keep moving! That's when we won't just be surviving, we'll be thriving.

Sandra Crawford Williamson
CEO of Crawford Creative Consulting
4word Advisory Board Member

Help Me

Because the Sovereign Lord helps me,
I will not be disgraced.

Isaiah 50:7

*L*eading from the heart. Doing what we believe is right. Choosing the road less travelled. Living true to yourself. Having faith in servant leadership.

We make choices every day, in what we say, what we do, and how we think. We take on challenges. And sometimes, no matter how hard we try, or how good our intentions may be, we simply find ourselves in uncomfortable, embarrassing, and perhaps even painfully difficult situations, be it at work, in our community, with our family, or even, with ourselves.

The words that come to mind are the "Lord helps me" in Isaiah 50. In reading this, we come to understand and trust that God is with us every step of the way. We're not standing alone. God is alongside us, as our rock and our shield.

Take a deep breath, know that He is with you, and He *will* see you through.

Evelyn M. Lee, PhD
Founder of Vocation Catalyst, Ltd.

Center Your Thoughts

Set your minds on things above, not on earthly things.

Colossians 3:2

*I*t was a typical Monday: late start, spilled coffee, bad attitude. I'd grown weary of the long commute to a job I disliked. I sat, stalled on the freeway with my thoughts swarming—hundreds of them, like unnerving co-passengers. They yelled frustrations with coworkers, honked holy expletives at my boss, chanted "early resignation!"

When my thoughts run amok, Christ, my patient passenger, beckons me, "Look in the rearview mirror. Your offenses are miles behind." I'm free to be with Him. My commute is meant for communion.

If I center my thoughts on Christ, I clear the way to life anew. This is a time to pray, confess, listen. Renewing my mind is a long journey, but I take a few steps forward each day on my commute. That's when my faithful copilot offers a timely traffic update: "Take your thoughts captive. It's the fastest route to freedom."

Brenda Bertrand
Speaker and Career Clarity Coach
4word Advisory Board Member

Fixing Stress
Is Stressful

The Lord is good, a strong refuge when trouble comes.
He is close to those who trust in him.

Nahum 1:7 NLT

*G*rowing up, I rarely encountered a problem I couldn't think or work my way out of. As a result, I developed a lot of confidence in my ability to handle whatever came my way. This confidence served me well in many ways, but it also led me to try to handle things myself that I should have been giving to God.

Stress is a great example. When I treat stress as just another problem for me to solve, I get in trouble, as in: ulcers, anxiety, resentment, and exhaustion. Working hard to fix your own stress is, well, stressful!

Serving and caring for other people gives me a healthy perspective of my own stress. It also pushes me to lean on God. He's bigger and stronger than we could ever imagine.

Diane Paddison
Founder of 4word women
Former Executive Team at Trammell Crow Company,
CBRE, and ProLogis

REFLECT & REFRESH

Are there parts of your story you are afraid to share? How might God use your story to help others?

Do you have too many plates spinning? Try asking for help, and allow God to bless you through others.

What part of your day can you dedicate to communion with God? Whether it's your commute, your lunch break, or a few minutes before the kids get up, dedicate that time to talking with and listening to God.

Lord, in my daily battle against stress and too many spinning plates, help me carve out time to spend with you. Show me which plates are worth keeping in the air and which need to fall. When I find myself overwhelmed, give me the humility to ask for help. You do not desire for me to live a stressed out, overworked life. Instead, you call me to abundant life with freedom from worry and stress. Teach me how to rest and put you first.

Week 25

Patient Love

Love does not delight in evil but rejoices with the truth.
It always protects, always trusts,
always hopes, always perseveres.

1 Corinthians 13:6–7

*D*istance makes the heart grow fonder? Maybe not, since distance also means you miss out on the "daily" of the other person's life, like church, meals, and talking through your day. Thankfully, while we dated long-distance, God helped us both focus on the positive. We were blessed to live in a time when we could touch base whenever we wanted through technology!

Distance does create more of a longing to see one another and to appreciate the times you do spend together. We feel it may have even helped us forgive one another a little more easily, because it was hard to be angry or upset with someone when you only get to spend a few hours each week together. The key to dating long-distance is to remember that it is a temporary trial. God's plans are greater than our own!

Serge and Anna Kalinin
Student
Product Manager at Amazon

Get Acclimated

Be filled with the Spirit, speaking to one another
with psalms, hymns, and songs from the Spirit.
Sing and make music from your heart to the Lord.

Ephesians 5:18-19

*L*et's be honest—unless you're a raging extrovert, plugging into a new church when you're single is not easy. I'm an extrovert, but being the new person, especially in a singles' group, can be daunting. As soon as possible, try to make at least one friend. Find someone else who's new like you and befriend her. Then you'll at least have a wingman!

Ultimately, the best way to connect in a new church is to simply dive in. Find a place to serve, show up for fellowships, and become a regular. Yes, you'll probably have to repeat your name over and over and initiate more conversations than you wish to. Eventually, though, you'll look around and realize that you're a part of a community that both needs and loves you, and one that you need and love as well.

Jessica Bufkin
Event Planner

Secret Marriage Recipe

Love is patient, love is kind. It does not envy,
it does not boast, it is not proud. It does not
dishonor others, it is not self-seeking, it is not
easily angered, it keeps no record of wrongs.

1 Corinthians 13:4–5

I don't cook. So when people ask for the secret recipe to a long, happy marriage, I giggle at the irony. The recipe is no secret. It boils down to both be pointed toward God.

How do you get there? Go to church and recharge to help get you through your workweek. Do life together with couples who serve as godly examples. Study God's Word together. Serve together (at church or elsewhere), which will strengthen your bond and increase unity.

Most importantly: pray together. Praying together is intimate. When my husband prays for me, I see him as my leader. I'm so in love with him for loving me.

What ingredients would you add to your marriage's secret recipe?

Lori Berry, MA-PC
Pastoral Counselor
4word Advisory Board Member

Deliberate Choices

Love and faithfulness meet together;
righteousness and peace kiss each other.

Psalm 85:10

*M*y husband and I met in college. We both knew that I would be in business and he would be in sports or education. That meant I would always have more earning potential than he did. We were very open about what each of us would have to deal with in terms of stereotypes and tough/annoying questions. In the end, we felt we could manage the difficulties, personally and publicly.

We found that the key is constant communication and deliberate choices. We take turns making sacrifices for each other's careers. Ultimately, what helps my husband helps me and vice versa. That is how God intended it. As each of us thrives, we bring that energy into the relationship. We try to keep focused on each other, although it can be very hard. Our perspective is that it is *our* marriage, *our* money, and *our* success.

Reagan Cannon
Leader, Speaker, and Author

Faith as Your Foundation

Walk by the Spirit, and you will not
gratify the desires of the flesh.

Galatians 5:16

Over the years, my husband, Chris, and I have each taken turns in the "breadwinner" role and in the primary caretaker role. We've each lost loved ones and seen our children through dark times. It hasn't always been easy, but we've found that the more ways we're able to devote time to God together, the better every facet of our relationship gets.

Try to establish a routine time where you and your husband are connecting with God and building your faith together. Chris and I try to pray together every day. We're also part of a couple's Bible study group at our church. Any time you can spend focusing on God together will help you align your priorities and perspectives. It helps me and Chris to see each other as teammates, with God at the center.

What does your marriage's foundation look like?

Diane Paddison
Founder of 4word women
Former Executive Team at Trammell Crow Company,
CBRE, and ProLogis

REFLECT & REFRESH

Are you connected at church? If not, what is one step you can take this week to dive in and serve?

If you are married, what is one ingredient for a happy marriage that you and your husband could add to your marriage "recipe"?

Are you or have you ever been the breadwinner in your family (or simply been the sole source of financial provision as a single woman)? How can you maintain the perspective that your money is not your own?

Lord, thank you for providing me with relationships that build me up and point me toward you. As iron sharpens iron, use my marriage to make me more Christlike each day, and help me do the same for my spouse. Help us be on the same page about finances and other major decisions that affect our relationship and our family. Help us put each other before ourselves. Most importantly, help us keep you at the center of our relationship, so our shared faith always remains the foundation of our marriage.

Week 26

Just Getting through It

And those who know Your name will
put their trust in You; For You, Lord,
have not forsaken those who seek You.

Psalm 9:10 NKJV

*O*ver the past few years, my family and I have been through many trials. Whenever we made it through a tough time, I prayerfully thanked God for getting us through. Lately, I've learned that perhaps the lesson He's been trying to drill into my head for years is not thankfulness that I'm *through*, but thankfulness that I was brought along on the journey.

The next time God deems me worthy to go through a dark time, I will thank Him for the honor and opportunity to learn from Him. Will I be scared? Will I cry a few tears of grief and anger? I'm human, so yes, probably. But I'm also committing to viewing life's hardships as God calling class into session and giving me the chance to discover the beauty behind the bad times.

Jordan Johnstone
Writer and Digital Community Manager for 4word

Fill the Vase

We have this treasure in jars of clay to show that
this all-surpassing power is from God and not from us.

2 Corinthians 4:7

*D*uring a trip to Chile, I bought a small clay vase as a keepsake. I carefully wrapped it in my clothes and placed it in the middle of my suitcase—only to find it smashed to pieces upon my return home.

It wasn't until months later, while reading in 2 Corinthians, that I realized my mistake. I'd failed to fill the *inside* of the vase to keep it from breaking. In that moment, God reminded me that I too am a clay jar, one that He formed. By failing to fill it with the Holy Spirit I am also in jeopardy of breaking. When I fill my soul with Him and His treasures, I'm transformed and strengthened with His all-surpassing power, prepared to face any situation, even the unexpected, whether in the office, at home, or abroad!

Shalyn Eyer
Leadership Consultant/Coach at FutureSense, LLC
4word Nashville Local Group Leader

Host of Obstacles

"For I am the Lord your God who takes hold of your
right hand and says to you, Do not fear; I will help you."

Isaiah 41:13

I never dreamed of being an entrepreneur, but that's the
path God planned for me. It's brought more challenges
and opportunities than any other in my career. No matter
what position you hold, there will always be obstacles that
impact your professional life—and test your faith.

When times were bad in the business, I often wondered
how much I needed to solve versus how much I should rely
on God to show me the way. Ten years later, I can tell you
God is always before you and alongside you, beckoning
you to follow Him. He goes ahead of you, opening up the
way, and stays close, never letting go of your right hand.
Your best path is trusting in the Lord and taking your troubles to Him, every time.

Tanya Hart Little
Founder and CEO of Hart Advisors Group, Hart Commercial,
and VistaPointe Partners

Take It to Him

Now to Him who is able to keep you from stumbling,
and to present you faultless before the presence
of His glory with exceeding joy.

Jude 24 NKJV

I love having a plan. I love preparing, organizing, anticipating the result, and seeing the fruition of my hard work. I expect, in an audience of career-driven women, I'm not alone in this! In our best-case scenario, everything works the way we expected, with no hiccups. But what about the worst-case scenario?

I've had to face challenges that made me feel deeply insecure in my abilities and/or uncertain of what to do next. God has shown me that while I may not be in control of those dreaded worst-case scenarios, He is.

Now, when a situation goes awry, I take it to Him in prayer. Without fail, He reorients my perspective and provides the wisdom needed to get me through difficult moments or decisions. I can count on Him in any situation, because He's the ultimate problem solver.

Emily Maloney
Attorney

Desperately Dependent

"The Lord will fight for you; you need only to be still."

Exodus 14:14

*B*y thirty-five, my life was looking pretty perfect—right up until the day I realized it was a fairy tale: pretty, cheerful, and not real.

My first thought was to try to save my marriage. When it became clear reconciliation wasn't possible, my focus shifted to my kids. Part of me wanted very much to hide: to close the door, wrap my sweet children in my arms, and shut the rest of the world out.

I didn't have that option. The world felt broken, but it didn't stop moving. So I kept putting one foot in front of the other. I kept going to work and to church. I leaned heavily on good friends and family and was deeply, desperately dependent on God.

Through it all, I saw and felt firsthand there is no pain and no trouble that God cannot redeem for His glory.

Diane Paddison
Founder of 4word women
Former Executive Team at Trammell Crow Company,
CBRE, and ProLogis

REFLECT & REFRESH

Are you journeying through a difficult season? Ask God to reveal the beauty of His presence and plan to you.

When you face major decisions at work or in your personal life, do you believe God is always before you and alongside you?

When you face a challenging problem or difficult situation this week, commit to take it to God in prayer before trying to tackle it on your own.

> Lord, I know that as hard as I try to make things run as smoothly as possible, I don't have control over every bump in the road that may come my way. I also know that through it all, you will be beside me. Help me remember to bring any challenge or trouble to you in prayer first, before trying to fix everything myself. Thank you for the beauty of your presence and your plan for my life in every circumstance. I believe that there is no pain or trouble that you cannot redeem for your glory.

Week 27

Know Your Purpose

The Lord will vindicate me; your love, Lord, endures forever—do not abandon the works of your hands.

Psalm 138:8

*W*e can become more connected in our church family by learning what we are gifted to do. Many times we don't know what God has purposed us to do, making it difficult to become involved. When you know your God-given purpose, you are in a better position to choose the ministry area best suited for you. God has given us all at least one gift; some of us more than one!

I believe the single most important factor is knowing your purpose. Pray to God with the specific purpose of learning what He would have you do. God will reveal the kingdom assignment that only you can do in His power and under His authority. I pray God will show each of us how to serve our church and how to minister not only to others but to ourselves.

Donna Renay Patrick
Author of *At All Times* and *It's in Your Praise*

Head Knowledge

But I trust in your unfailing love; my heart rejoices
in your salvation. I will sing the Lord's praise,
for he has been good to me

Psalm 13:5–6

I'm a born-and-raised Oregonian who moved to a small town in Montana when my husband took a new job. It was a big move for us, being newly married, and my first time permanently living away from family and friends back home. I was blessed by a supportive boss who allowed me to keep working remotely after we moved. Then, we embarked on another new adventure—welcoming a baby girl!

It's been a season of transition, but one I'm thankful for as God has used it to strengthen my faith. Having the "head knowledge" that God always provides for our needs, but learning to trust Him to do that in my own life, has been one of the biggest challenges and blessings of this season. I eagerly await what He has in store for us next!

Caitie Butler
4word Church Connect Program Manager

Feeling Like an Outsider

You are the body of Christ,
and each one of you is a part of it.

1 Corinthians 12:27

*H*ow can professional Christian women start to feel like they *belong* in their church family?

We need to reevaluate our routines. We want to sit near our friends, hear worship music we like, and listen to a message that resonates with us where we are. It's true that we go to church to learn about God's Word and to worship Him on a very personal level. But part of the blessing of the local church is our growth as a community.

If you feel like an outsider, reach out to other women at church who walk in shoes similar to yours. Form a small group or after-work study. Church is a place built on love and compassion for each other. Let's put that into action in our lives.

Diane Paddison
Founder of 4word women
Former Executive Team at Trammell Crow Company,
CBRE, and ProLogis

Take Up Your Mat

He said to the man, "I tell you, get up,
take your mat and go home." He got up, took
his mat and walked out in full view of them all.

Mark 2:10–12

Throughout Jesus' ministry, He surprised us. I hope to be just like that, surprising people with love and grace to the glory of God. To do this, I must be willing to step out in faith.

Jesus' miracle in Mark 2:1–12 is twofold—He forgives the man's sins and restores his body, then challenges him to pick up his mat and walk. It's significant that Jesus asked him to walk, in front of everyone, into the community. The once-paralyzed man, now walking, is a clear picture to those around him of Jesus' power.

What has Jesus done for you? He's forgiven your sins and restores you each day. Are you "taking up your mat and walking" in full view of the world?

Lauren Ford
Young Life Capernaum Director

Walking with Jesus

*"Silver or gold I do not have,
but what I do have I give you."*

Acts 3:6

I'd like to share what I think is the key to a full life: an abiding, growing, and central relationship with God. I titled my first book *Walking with Jesus in Healthcare,* because walking with Jesus will always lead us to God's best for our lives.

As we stay close to our Shepherd, we discover safe pastures and living waters. Walking with Jesus is not merely a *good* decision, it's the *best* decision we can ever make, for the dividends of this relationship are eternal. I love helping people grow closer to God and to their God-given purpose. Like Peter said in Acts 3:6, "Silver or gold I do not have, but what I do have I give you." What I have is the love and power of Christ, and that's the best thing I can share with anyone.

Amaryllis Sánchez Wohlever, MD
Physician, Wellness, and Burnout Coach

REFLECT & REFRESH

What gifts do you believe God has equipped you with that you can use to serve your family, your workplace, and the church?

Do you ever feel like an outsider in your church? If so, what steps can you take to find community with other women?

What can you do to "take up your mat and walk" today?

Lord, thank you for equipping me with unique gifts that allow me to serve those around me. Help me remember that I am your hands and feet in my workplace, home, church, and community. I commit to taking the "head knowledge" I have about you and putting it into practice, trusting you to give me opportunities to use my gifts, and to share your love with those around me. Give me courage to "take up my mat" so your power will shine through me.

Week 28

Jesus' Leadership Secrets

He replied, "You of little faith, why are you so afraid?"
Then he got up and rebuked the winds
and the waves, and it was completely calm.

Matthew 8:26

*W*ould you choose Jesus to run your company? When we think about Jesus, we tend to focus on His humility, compassion, and sacrifice—traits we should all strive to bring to the workplace. Yet there's also a lot to learn from the practical ways Jesus led His team.

In a relatively short time, Jesus called together an unlikely group of men, built them up, and inspired them to literally change the world. Jesus loved His disciples, but He cared more about their development and their purpose than their immediate comfort.

I know I can do my best in the workplace if I look to the example Christ Jesus set for us, and try to lead people similarly to how Christ Himself led others.

Diane Paddison
Founder of 4word women
Former Executive Team at Trammell Crow Company,
CBRE, and ProLogis

Conviction under Pressure

We rejoice in our sufferings, knowing that
suffering produces endurance,

Romans 5:3 ESV

*A*t the beginning of every year, I set an exercise goal
to work on my physical fitness. One year, I actually
stuck with it. After several months, I noticed the results of
the many hours I endured going up and down imaginary
hills in spin class. My reflection showed off my hard work.

Life's trials can sometimes feel like spin class. During
one difficult time, I had a boss who would throw out a
"fresh" new idea and I'd think to myself, *I just said that.* Life
became too difficult for me to even smile. However, God
taught me a valuable lesson.

I learned that God uses life's difficult times to teach us
how to hold on to our Christian convictions under pressure. In other words, trials develop our spiritual fitness.
Consequently, after months of enduring spiritual "spin
class," when I noticed that my character reflected newly
formed spiritual muscle, I ... smiled.

Irrayna Uribe
Executive Director for Virtuous Communications, Inc.

On and Off Ramps

Though one may be overpowered,
two can defend themselves.
A cord of three strands is not quickly broken.

Ecclesiastes 4:12

Whether you're a stay-at-home mom or work full-time, you will be challenged as to the choices you've made for you and your family. Many women are not able to stay at home for financial reasons. Women who love their careers choose to go back to work because they enjoy it—and that doesn't mean they love their children any less. We can all be better moms by supporting one another, knowing we're teaching our children as they observe our interactions with other women.

Ladies, support one another and get advice from other godly women who've had to make decisions similar to the ones you face. Remember, as women we'll have on and off ramps throughout our career. Seek God's will for you and your family, and have confidence in the path He's chosen for you.

Meghan Dion
Full-time Wife and Mother

Self-Condemnation

*Indeed, there is no one on earth who is righteous,
no one who does what is right and never sins.*

Ecclesiastes 7:20

The driving force behind many accomplished women is a spirit and pursuit of excellence. This helps us achieve great things, but it can also be our biggest spiritual challenge!

Our need to be perfect in all we do can foster self-condemnation, a spirit of striving, not resting, and a lack of the joy and peace that we're called to in Christ. Our identity cannot be in the things we achieve—it must be in Christ.

It's hard to let go of the world's evaluation of who we are, and to fully embrace the peace, joy, and affirmation that come from being a daughter of Christ—nothing more, nothing less. Christ doesn't love me any more or less if I excel at work every minute of every day. How much freedom could we experience if we actually loved ourselves that same way?

Sheeba Philip
VP of Marketing Strategy & Communications, JCPenney

Bring Peace

She held court under the Palm of Deborah between
Ramah and Bethel in the hill country of Ephraim,
and the Israelites went up to her
to have their disputes decided.

Judges 4:5

What makes a good leader? One amazing leader is Deborah. She was a prophet. She led Israel. She'd been given full authority over all the people and didn't shy away from it. There didn't seem to be a question about her being in charge. The people believed God had provided her as a leader, so they followed her and came to her. Deborah wasn't chasing anything that hadn't already been given to her.

Deborah believed God, accepted authority, exercised discernment, valued people, empowered leaders, listened to God, loved peace, showed up when it was time to fight, and praised God. Her story ends: "Then the land had peace forty years" (Judges 5:31).

Does your office, home, or church need a "Deborah"— like you?

Lori Berry, MA-PC
Pastoral Counselor
4word Advisory Board Member

REFLECT & REFRESH

What is one thing you can do to improve your spiritual fitness this week?

Have you ever felt guilty over a decision you've made, such as the decision to stay at home or go back to work?

Do you believe God loves you regardless of how you perform at work, simply because you are His daughter? How does/would that belief change your perception of yourself?

Lord, thank you for calling me to be a leader in my sphere of influence—at home, at work, at church, and in my community. Thank you for the trials and challenges you've allowed me to go through and used to strengthen my faith. Help me be disciplined in my pursuit of you. When I feel like I've fallen short at work or at home, remind me that I'm your daughter and that your love for me is not depen-dent on my performance. Give me confidence in the decisions I've made and help me stay aligned with your will, regardless of the opinions of others.

Week 29

Seeking Order

Everything should be done in a fitting and orderly way.

1 Corinthians 14:40

I'm a stacker. There are towers of plastic bins in my house filled with VBS crafts I will never scrapbook, T-shirts I will never quilt, and business articles I will never read. I'm not proud of my stacking. I used to feel alone, until I said something. It turns out there are many of us "stackers" out there.

God is a God of order. Just consider how He created the world. As His daughters, are we following in His organizational footsteps? Here are a few tips to help us get started: 1) *Declare war* on the stacks and recruit help, 2) Don't wait for a sale at the Container Store®, *start now*, 3) *Let it go*–Craigslist® will only add another step, and 4) Clutter multiplies, so *fight the battle daily*.

Embarrassment isn't from the Lord. Stewardship, order, and grace *are*. Let's pray for God's help to stamp out the stacker in all of us.

Sandra Crawford Williamson
CEO of Crawford Creative Consulting
4word Advisory Board Member

Choose to Give

*"Give, and it will be given to you. A good measure,
pressed down, shaken together and running over,
will be poured into your lap. For with the measure you
use, it will be measured to you."*

Luke 6:38

God is an amazing giver, and He wants us to be more like Him in giving. Of course, that's not the nature of the world in which we live. We live and work in a place that's the opposite of God's giving principle. Giving generously really comes down to trust. By trusting God's principle rather than our nature, we can learn to let this principle become our *new* nature.

When you think about becoming a better giver, try to think about more than money and possessions. Think about other areas where you may lean into being selfish. Are you selfish in your habits, relationships, attitudes, or time? Ask God to show you the areas in which He wants you to grow and help you to become a better giver.

Lisa Creed
Owner of Good News Coaching

Start with Gratitude

I will give thanks to you, Lord, with all my heart;
I will tell of all your wonderful deeds.

Psalm 9:1

*F*ocusing on gratitude has changed my life. Yes, being a working mom with young children means there are a lot of things to balance, and there is stress. But when I approach each day from the perspective of being thankful to God for my blessings, it fills me with a sense of peace that enables me to handle whatever the day brings.

Every morning before I take out the dog, get the kids ready for school, check my email, or stress about a big meeting, I pray, "Dear Lord—thank you for all the blessings you have given me. Thank you for my health, family, friends, and job. Thank you that I get to do work that is meaningful to me, provide for my family, and help others." Start your day with gratitude to God—it will change your life!

Jaxie Alt
Senior Vice President of Marketing, Dr Pepper Snapple Group

Preach without Words

"Whoever wants to become great among you
must be your servant, and whoever wants
to be first must be slave of all."

Mark 10:43–44

*S*ervant leadership is one of my core principles, but I don't often talk about it. I want it quietly demonstrated by how I handle challenges and how I treat others. I'm often reminded of the words attributed to Francis of Assisi: "Preach Jesus, and if necessary use words."

I strive to err on the side of generosity. If you believe in people before they even believe in themselves, they often rise to the level of expectation sooner than if you're dogmatic about guidelines.

In my years as a CEO, I've found generosity engenders a culture of people helping and encouraging one another all the way down the line. People want someone to believe in them. Be the one who helps give them the confidence they need!

Erin Botsford
CEO of Botsford Financial Group
Author of *The Big Retirement Risk: Running out
of Money before You Run out of Time*
4word Board Member

Rags to Riches

*Though he was rich, yet for your sakes he became poor,
so that by his poverty he could make you rich.*

2 Corinthians 8:9 NLT

*A*s women in the workplace, we often dedicate much of our time to thinking about money: budgets (at work and at home), investments, and payroll. The Bible talks about a different kind of wealth. As followers of Jesus, we're asked to put aside the riches of the world in order to inherit God's best for us, in this life and in eternity.

The apostle Paul was someone who went from riches to rags, giving up his immense wealth and power to follow Jesus. The Lord blessed him with one of the richest lives imaginable.

However, according to 2 Corinthians 8:9, Jesus led the ultimate "riches to rags" life. The more we focus on Jesus, the more we'll follow His example of rich generosity.

Diane Paddison
Founder of 4word women
Former Executive Team at Trammell Crow Company,
CBRE, and ProLogis

REFLECT & REFRESH

What is one area of your life where you could become a better giver? Are you selfish in your habits, relationships, attitudes, or time?

Challenge yourself to start tomorrow with gratitude. Before diving into your to-do list, stop and thank God for the blessings you've been given.

How can you foster a culture of encouragement in your workplace?

Lord, thank you for the many riches I have been given, not just financially, but through my family, friendships, and opportunities to use the gifts and talents you've given me in the workplace. Help me foster a spirit of generosity and thankfulness, instead of selfishness. I want to live with open hands, ready to freely give from the deep well of blessings I have been given. When I walk through a difficult season, help me to maintain a grateful heart and give freely. I want to always be a good steward of the resources you have given me.

Week 30

Achiever Racer

But godliness with contentment is great gain.

1 Timothy 6:6

I have cerebral palsy. However, this has never kept me
from living a fulfilled, joyful, and positive life as a student, professional woman, and now in volunteering during
my retirement years. My zeal for life is because I love to
accomplish long-term goals. Although the Lord has blessed
me with a realistic positive determination in reaching those
goals, it was the encouragement of wise parents, a caring
brother, and precious friends that provided the fuel to ignite
my "achiever racer" spirit.

Now, in my retirement years, I continue to run a race
toward a goal. Pursuing life in Christ is a goal that will not
finish until I put a foot in heaven. I hope I begin my life in
my heavenly home by hearing "Well done, faithful servant.
You have used the gifts given to you."

Evey Wysocki
Retired Assistant Manager of the Rent & Mortgage Dept.
in the office of the VP of Finance at Princeton University

Promised Land

As he was praying, the appearance of his face changed,
and his clothes became as bright as a flash
of lightning. Two men, Moses and Elijah, appeared
in glorious splendor, talking with Jesus.

Luke 9:29–30

Sometimes, God says no to His children. We're in good company when it comes to receiving this answer. God told Moses he wouldn't enter the Promised Land and Paul that He wouldn't remove the "thorn." God even told His own Son He wouldn't be spared the cross.

Moses' life's dream was to enter the Promised Land. Between Deuteronomy 3 and 34, we see Moses become a changed man. He clearly heard God's resounding no, yet his last words were in blessing and praise of God.

God's no gives way to His better yes. It was Moses who stood, *fully in the Promised Land* at the Transfiguration, and spoke with Jesus regarding the cross. *The cross.* This was Moses' inconceivable, glorious yes! Our yes waits on our acceptance.

Suzanne Matthews
Author of *Unlocking Belief: Answering Questions Jesus Asks*

Need for Healing

Lord my God, I called to you for help,
and you healed me.

Psalm 30:2

"Mi Sheberach imoteinu M'kor habrachah laavoteinu—Bless those in need of healing with r'fuah sh'leimah, the renewal of body, the renewal of spirit."

In Judaism, we say this prayer, called a "Mi Sheberach," for those in need of healing. It is used for people who need healing physically, spiritually, or emotionally. It is a public prayer, said as part of a community, and sometimes the name of the person being prayed for is said aloud. It comforts those who are concerned for the person in need of healing, as well as the one who is ailing. And it puts the community in the position of supporting those who say the prayer, as they all say it together.

Is there anyone in need of healing who you can pray for today?

Carol Fishman Cohen
CEO of iRelaunch

Rejoicing Sorrow

Sorrowful, yet always rejoicing; poor,
yet making many rich; having nothing,
and yet possessing everything.

2 Corinthians 6:10

I've never gone through anything as horrible as watching my daughter, Annie, suffer through months of debilitating pain. I've experienced suffering before—a divorce, a rebellious teenager, the loss of my parents—but this tops it all.

In the beginning, I cried out to God, "Why my daughter? Why my family? Why me?" My cries and questioning led me to an important central question.

The pain we experience in life forces us to turn to God, because pain won't be ignored. By allowing pain, God makes people aware of their need for Him. Then, God demonstrates His benevolence through suffering by allowing us to actually experience contentment and happiness through obedience and submission to His will. If we learn to obey our intrinsically good God, then we will receive the blessing upon blessing through that obedience.

Diane Paddison
Founder of 4word women
Former Executive Team at Trammell Crow Company,
CBRE, and ProLogis

Private Faith?

*Do your best to present yourself to God as
one approved, a worker who does not need to be
ashamed and who correctly handles the word of truth.*

2 Timothy 2:15

There's a general misunderstanding that all aspects of our faith need to be private. It's as though there's an unwritten social rule that politics and business can be public conversation, but faith—this thing that connects to the core of who we really are—*that* needs to be kept under lock and key, consigned to the closet.

Our faith, in the normal expression of daily life, was always meant to be lived with a watching world in view. Jesus said it best when He compared the public outworking of our faith in service to others as lights that were never meant to be hidden (Matthew 5:15). Instead, they should be well positioned, so that people can see them more clearly. When the world sees this, they see God's creative handiwork in action. That handiwork is you!

Steve Haas
Catalyst—World Vision

REFLECT & REFRESH

Have you experienced a time when pain, whether physical or emotional, caused you to turn to God?

Has God recently told you "no" or "not yet" to your desires? Ask God for patience as you wait on His best "yes."

How can you be a "shining light on a hill" at work this week?

Lord, I praise you for your sovereignty over my life, in both the times of blessing and the times of suffering. I know you are good, and you have a perfect plan for my life. I trust you to lead me, accepting your "no" and "not yet" as I wait on your best "yes" for me. When I am tempted to forge my own path, remind me that waiting on you is always the best thing for my life. May my trust in you shine outward, so that others can see and know your goodness.

Week 31

Your Legacy

Children are a heritage from the Lord;
offspring are a blessing from him.

Psalm 127:3

*W*hat is my legacy? The Lord has given me myriad talents and resources to enrich my worlds—corporate leading and coaching, as well as sharing my energy and passion for women in the workplace.

But I know that my successes in these areas pale by comparison to my role in guiding my children and my children's children to God. I pray God would help me to creatively and lovingly support them in their careers, marriages, and parenting adventures. I pray my legacy will be all the roles God created me to fill—my positions in the marketplace, my impact on workingwomen, and my critical role in every child's life with whom God has blessed me.

What kind of legacy are you leaving? Ask God to help you focus on how best you can leave your mark on this world.

Patricia Myers
Former Director, Talent Management
Director, Leadership Development for National Commercial
Bank of Saudi Arabia (NCB)
Executive Coach and 4word Board Member

The Lonely Journey

*Fathers, do not exasperate your children;
instead, bring them up in the training
and instruction of the Lord.*

Ephesians 6:4

Josh came to us at nine years old from a very difficult situation. He provided significant challenges, taking our family to places we knew nothing about. The juvenile justice system. Repeated visits to traffic court. Jail and the hospital. Friends who lied to, stole from, took advantage of, and abused us and our home.

By God's grace, our family came through it all in peace and love. Josh even had a positive impact on our ministry. We didn't hide our struggle. We lived out the journey in appropriate ways before our staff, and found new doors of ministry opened.

Parents, I know your journey sometimes feels lonely and endlessly trying. God places us in these "iron sharpening" situations to not only become the parents our children need but the child He wants us to be. Draw close to your heavenly Father, so your children will draw close to you.

Judy Douglass
Writer, Speaker, Encourager

Open Up

Being confident of this, that he who began
a good work in you will carry it on to completion
until the day of Christ Jesus.

Philippians 1:6

*G*oing through fertility issues can feel incredibly lonely. The feeling of shame adds to the isolation. As a driven corporate woman, I found it hard to be in a situation I couldn't control. No amount of research, work, or money could fix the problem. Fearing I'd be viewed as weak, I refused to open up about my struggle.

At times like this, even our spouses might not know how to support us. Some days, I know I made it all about me. But God would remind me this was something we were going through together.

To anyone going through an infertility journey, I implore you to open up. Connect with those around you. Seek out a support group of other women—a group who'll accept any feeling or thought of yours, and help you surrender it to God's will.

Sandra Crawford Williamson
CEO of Crawford Creative Consulting
4word Advisory Board Member

Be Their Cheerleader

Encourage each other and build each other up,
just as you are already doing.

1 Thessalonians 5:11 NLT

I'm so grateful for the confidence that both of my parents built in me from a young age. Like most parents of daughters, they told me I was beautiful, but they also showed me I was powerful.

My dad developed my confidence by giving me more and more responsibility on the farm. He had me waiting on customers at our retail stand by ten years old. In my early teens, I ran the peach thinning crew. By sixteen, I was leading crews of twenty, picking peaches. I was blessed to have a dad and mom that always supported and expected me to do bigger and bigger things.

Parents, be your child's cheerleader, but don't be a crutch. Set them up to naturally discover their own confidence, and be prepared to encourage when a situation goes astray.

Diane Paddison
Founder of 4word women
Former Executive Team at Trammell Crow Company,
CBRE, and ProLogis

Exercise Caution

Each person is tempted when they are dragged
away by their own evil desire and enticed.

James 1:14

I take extreme measures to avoid Girl Scouts in February. When the doorbell rings, I dive and roll. When they have a table set up at the grocery store, I take an alternate entrance.

You see, I have a weakness. One bite into peanut butter and chocolate deliciousness, and the whole box is gone. Then I look for another box. Not long afterward, I feel really, really sick and angry with myself for thinking I could eat just one (again).

What do you need to take extreme measures to avoid? That guy at work who thinks you're awesome? Charging in to take over for your kid? That first glass of wine? The store that has everything you "need"? That first self-destructive, negative thought?

Don't fall for "just one bite" again. Choose what's better. Walk in the side entrance. Dive and roll.

Lori Berry, MA-PC
Pastoral Counselor
4word Advisory Board Member

REFLECT & REFRESH

If you have children, find one way to encourage them in their faith this week.

What kind of legacy are you leaving? Ask God to help you focus on how you can best leave your mark on this world.

Is there an unhealthy habit you need to "dive and roll" from? Take the first step and decide to choose what's better.

Lord, thank you for giving me the opportunity to not only live for you in this life, but to build a legacy that points people toward you for generations to come. Help me grow more like you each day as I serve my children and grandchildren, or prepare for those who will come under my care in the future. Show me areas of weakness in my life that I need to turn away from and avoid at all costs, so I can live in your freedom. I want to be the best example of a woman after your heart as I can, for my family and those coming up behind me.

Week 32

Little White Lie

Do not lie to each other, since you have taken off your
old self with its practices and have put on the new self.

Colossians 3:9–10

*H*ow often do you feel tempted to polish the truth at
work? Lying is a learned behavior: the more you
practice it, the better you'll be. Almost nothing is more
damaging to your professional reputation than becoming
known as dishonest.

Cultivating a reputation for honesty isn't always easy,
but it can pay huge dividends. The next time you're
tempted to tell a "little white lie" to your boss, or feel the
need to exaggerate the ease of a project to coworkers to
gain a few brownie points, take the time to decide if risking your reputation, and God's, is really worth the minor
reward in the end. Ask God to remove the temptation of
the "little white lie" from your heart on a daily basis.

Diane Paddison
Founder of 4word women
Former Executive Team at Trammell Crow Company,
CBRE, and ProLogis

Weight of Anxiety

Anxiety weighs down the heart,
but a kind word cheers it up.

Proverbs 12:25

*E*verything I've accomplished in my personal life, as well as with our nonprofit, always begins with a challenge. Because of this, I view every problem that arises as temporary instead of permanent.

Many people try to apply a permanent solution to a temporary problem in their life. When you're presented with a challenge of any size, don't feel like you have to address it immediately. Take a step back, pray, and seek counsel from those you trust. You never know the variety of options available to you to combat your problem until you seek them out.

Learn and understand who Christ is in your life. When He becomes the center of all you do, you'll have the assurance inside that you're not on this earth to please others. You are here to please God. At the end, that's all that will ever matter.

Ceitci Demirkova
Founder and CEO of Changing a Generation

Clean Hands

Who may ascend the mountain of the Lord?
Who may stand in his holy place? The one who
has clean hands and a pure heart, who does not
trust in an idol or swear by a false god.
They will receive blessing from the Lord.

Psalm 24:3-5

My mom was continually asking, "Did you wash your hands?" Clean hands were important to her, because polio, smallpox, and the great flu epidemic greatly impacted her generation. Clean hands help prevent the spread of disease.

It was the Jewish custom to ceremonially wash your hands before eating; hands had to be "baptized." When people finish a frustrating project, they say, "I've washed my hands of the matter." When someone wants to declare their innocence, they proclaim, "My hands are clean."

As we start each day, let us stand before the Lord and pray for clean hands and pure hearts, so we can serve Him and know the blessings He has for us.

Commissioner Debi Bell
Territorial President of Women's Ministries, The Salvation Army,
USA Southern Territory

Approaching Conflict

"I have told you these things, so that in me you may have peace. In this world you will have trouble. But take heart! I have overcome the world."

John 16:33

Scripture tells us we'll have conflict in life. It's how we handle the conflict that matters. How can we ease tension in the workplace? How do we approach conflict in a Christian way?

First, we talk directly to the person with whom we're struggling. How we approach a person sets the tone for the whole conversation. I start with common ground. I confess my part in the current issue and ask the other person to forgive me. Remember, the goal of the conversation is to preserve the relationship, not to "win" the battle.

No conflict is worth sacrificing our ability to perform the duties we've been hired to carry out. A few moments of discomfort and transparency will result in a more unified work relationship, improving the performance of everyone involved.

Lori Berry, MA-PC
Pastoral Counselor
4word Advisory Board Member

Refined by Fire

"Do not fear, for I have redeemed you;
I have summoned you by name; you are mine.
When you walk through the fire, you will not be burned;
the flames will not set you ablaze."

Isaiah 43:1–2

I am a woman, a mother, a wife, an educator, and a survivor of domestic abuse. Years ago, I lived in a beachfront home surrounded by beauty and affluence. But no matter how beautiful our view and our home, it couldn't fix the pain behind our locked doors. I felt alone and unloved, but I was not. God always loved me. He was working in that pain and that fear, and He was purposing me to help women impacted by abuse.

I named my organization *Stronger than Espresso*, because espresso is intensely strong coffee, made under pressure and with extreme heat. We're women refined by fire. We are fierce, and fiercely loved by a God who strengthens and provides.

Dr. Brooke Jones
Founder of Stronger than Espresso

REFLECT & REFRESH

Have you ever "polished the truth" at work? Commit to being honest in both the big and little things.

Are you facing conflict in your workplace? Ask God for wisdom and courage, and then take the first step in resolving the conflict today.

This week, start each day by praying for clean hands and a pure heart.

> Lord, I admit that I often fall short in walking with integrity as you have called me to do. When I am tempted by the ways of the world to tell a white lie or admit my role in causing conflict, give me wisdom to live out your command to be honest and put others before myself. I trust you to go before me and bless my desire to be a woman with integrity. Remind me that my value comes directly from you and your love for me, not from the praise of others. Teach me to be a woman after your heart.

Week 33

God's Guiding Lights

Plans fail for lack of counsel,
but with many advisers they succeed.

Proverbs 15:22

*F*ew people have had more of an impact on my personal and professional development than my mentor, Diane Paddison. Several years ago, I graduated from Harvard Business School and was a young African American associate at Trammell Crow Company where Diane was a division president. Diane was well-known for her passion toward diversity, talent development, and connecting believers in the company.

Diane not only encouraged me to realize my full potential at work, but to see God's hand in the path ahead of me. At thirty-five, I had a senior leadership position that could have been challenging. I would have succumbed to at least a dozen traps, but Diane coached me on leadership effectiveness, navigating corporate politics, and most of all, having faith in God's purpose for me when times got tough. Mentors, in my opinion, are God's guiding lights on His path for your life.

Craig Robinson
CEO of Global Corporate Services
at Newmark Grubb Knight Frank (NGKF)

There Is No "Enough"

If it is serving, then serve;
if it is teaching, then teach.

Romans 12:7

*A*while back, I was given the opportunity to serve as a mentor in the 4word Mentor Program. My initial reaction was, "Me? I can't be a mentor!" I wasn't that far into my career and felt I had nothing to offer. But I stepped out in faith and said "yes"—and proceeded to have one of the most amazing experiences of my life. At the end of our time together, I couldn't believe I was so close to saying "no" to this gift from God.

Don't make the mistake I almost did. There's no "enough" level to measure your eligibility to help others. God can, and does, use anyone to be an instrument for His children. When we doubt our abilities, we doubt His plan. Mentorship is not a scary or pretentious thing. It's an opportunity for two individuals to come together and pour into each other's lives.

Jordan Johnstone
Writer and Digital Community Manager for 4word

Free to Receive

And if by grace, then it cannot be based on works;
if it were, grace would no longer be grace.

Romans 11:6

From Bible study groups to Pokeno groups, I surround myself with women who can speak wisdom into me. My all-time favorite advice came from a mentor who'd raised four kids a few years older than mine. She regularly reminded me, "This too shall pass." When you're in the trenches, you need to be reminded your season will change.

To me, walking in freedom is the difference between being saved, but holding onto your sin, guilt, bitterness, negativity, and anger, versus being free of all those things because of *grace*. When I finally learned to forgive myself and others, I was *free* to receive and give grace.

Who can you speak wisdom into today? Remind someone that walking in freedom is something we're all able to enjoy. Grace is just waiting for us to reach out and claim!

Lori Berry, MA-PC
Pastoral Counselor
4word Advisory Board Member

Be a Naomi

"Where you go I will go, and where you stay, I will stay.
Your people will be my people and your God my God."

Ruth 1:16

*W*e need mentors, and we need to mentor others. No matter where we are in our personal and professional lives, life can get hard. We were not designed to go through this life alone. We have a need for identity and belonging. We need the wisdom of those who are wiser to help us persevere when we don't know where we are going.

When disaster struck, Naomi was a faithful guide and mentor to Ruth. As they journeyed through life together, they began to learn from and lean on each other. I have discovered the beauty of mentoring, and that is why I invite others to commit to mentoring relationships. This is God's gift to us.

Natasha Sistrunk Robinson
Author of *Mentor for Life: Finding Purpose through Intentional Discipleship*

Pay It Forward

May these words of my mouth and this
meditation of my heart be pleasing in your sight,
Lord, my Rock and my Redeemer.

Psalm 19:14

"*Paying it forward*" is my passion. Is it yours? When you meet a younger woman, consider, "Can I help in any way?" Ask yourself how you can best help her, whether she's looking for a new opportunity, struggling to find meaning or purpose in her job, or weighing a difficult decision. Sharing our stories and offering encouragement is never a burden, and will help other women in ways you can't imagine.

Seek the women ahead of and behind you who can walk with you through trials, or who need your love and encouragement during a difficult time. I pray we all have eyes to see the women in our lives who need to hear our stories of grace and redemption in our homes and workplaces.

Diane Paddison
Founder of 4word women
Former Executive Team at Trammell Crow Company,
CBRE, and ProLogis

REFLECT & REFRESH

Do you have a mentor walking with you in your current season of life? If not, pray for guidance and take the first step in reaching out to a potential mentor this week.

Have you ever felt too inadequate to be a mentor? Ask God to show you how you can offer wisdom and guidance to another woman in your life.

Who can you speak wisdom to today? Pray for eyes to see those who need a reminder of God's grace and freedom.

Lord, thank you that I do not have to walk alone. When I am in need of wisdom and guidance, show me the women you've placed in my life who I can go to for advice. Give me eyes to see younger women coming up behind me who need a little encouragement, and give me confidence in my ability to be a mentor, even when I feel inadequate. I know that your Spirit will guide me in my mentoring relationships as I seek you.

Week 34

Your Core

Live in harmony with each other.
Don't be too proud to enjoy the company of
ordinary people. And don't think you know it all!

Romans 12:16 NLT

My family, friends, and faith community were the core of my marriage process and outcome. Once I recognized that God had given me a crowd who loved me the most and knew me the best, I knew I could rely on them to help me make one of the most important decisions in life.

There are family, friends, church buddies, mentors, coworkers, life group members, and many more people God has put right in front of you. These communities are important to so many aspects of life, including practical, spiritual, professional, intellectual, and our emotional needs and growth. Being intentional about your relationships helps to strengthen these aspects of community. As we live authentically with others, we learn to trust and include them as we pursue our dreams and desires.

Sharla Langston
Engagement Team of Generous Giving

Live Stronger

Be devoted to one another in love.
Honor one another above yourselves.

Romans 12:10

hat is most difficult in any conflict scenario is listening with the intention of truly understanding. Our brains work in such a way that as soon as a topic is thrown out, our mind has already decided on it. It's a natural human defense mechanism.

But remember, a person's conclusion on a topic is based on their own experiences with that topic. We are each a product of our past, and your own experiences might have been completely different. Allow yourself the gift of exploring life through someone else's view and perspective. God has given us a path laid out specifically for each of us, but in sharing our individual stories we gain strength and understanding.

Respecting someone else's opinion does not mean you must change yours. It allows you the opportunity to live stronger in your own thoughts and faith.

Fabi Howard, MA, LPC
Speaker & Professional Coach at Living StrongHer

Don't Live in Isolation

How good and pleasant it is when God's
people live together in unity!

Psalm 133:3

*O*ne summer, I took a job scraping paint off an old house. It was just another girl and me, scraping away. It was hot, humid, and very hard work. But it wasn't so bad, because I had someone with whom to laugh and sing. One day she couldn't make it and I was alone. That day seemed so incredibly long, and somehow it felt hotter.

The Christian life is hot, humid, and hard. We need people around us reminding us of our purpose here on this earth. We need people to speak the truth when lies are prevalent in our minds and we need to do the same for those around us.

Remember, God didn't create us to live in isolation. We are meant to be in community.

Sandra Crawford Williamson
CEO of Crawford Creative Consulting
4word Advisory Board Member

Obey the Call

God places the lonely in families.

Psalm 68:6 NLT

I met Melody Dulin at church. She noticed my loneliness and invited me to spend Thanksgiving with her family. At first, I declined. After all, I was a strong, independent woman. But Melody was persistent and said God told her to invite me.

Today, I call these extraordinary, righteous, godly people my "holy family." They are a gift and whatever God gives is holy. I now enjoy being seated at their family table at birthdays, weddings, and holidays.

We are all lost and alone without faith, searching for what is missing, but confused and afraid to take steps that might be embarrassing. Then one day, we obey the call of Jesus. We are adopted into His family with the full rights of heirs of His kingdom. We are daughters of the King, and nothing we can do can dissuade His love for us.

Kelly McDermott Thurman
Former Global Head of Sales for EDS
Managing Partner AdviSoar
4word Chair of the Board

Sharpened Iron

As iron sharpens iron, so a friend sharpens a friend.

Proverbs 27:17 NLT

For workingwomen with countless demands on their lives, friendship often gets pushed to the side. But we can't treat friends like a hobby. Friends are an integral part of God's plan for our lives.

Be intentional about forming and building solid Christian friendships. Like any other relationship, true friendship requires an investment of time and energy. But this investment yields unbelievable dividends. Through relationship one woman sharpens another. Healthy, supportive relationships with other Christian women will positively impact almost every area of your life.

Wherever you are in your friendship journey, I encourage you to stick with it. Make the time, even when it feels like there isn't any. Put in the effort, even when it feels like too much. Keep seeking connection, even when it feels awkward. Do these things for your benefit, but also for the benefit of your (future) friends.

Diane Paddison
Founder of 4word women
Former Executive Team at Trammell Crow Company,
CBRE, and ProLogis

REFLECT & REFRESH

Who do you consider your community or your "home team"? How has God used them to guide you in life?

Think of a recent conflict you faced at work. How did your past experiences shape how you handled that conflict?

Find someone who needs a friend this week. Invite that person to coffee or lunch, and ask God to use you to be an encouragement.

Lord, thank you that I don't have to walk this "hot, humid, and hard" life alone. Thank you for the community you have surrounded me with through friends, family, coworkers, and church. When I feel lonely and isolated, bring people across my path who are willing to reach out and encourage me, and help me have eyes to see others who need the same gift of friendship. Give me courage and boldness to reach out and ask for friendship and encouragement when I need it, knowing that your desire for me is to live in community with other people who love you.

Week 35

Wait Patiently

*As the heavens are higher than the earth,
so are my ways higher than your ways
and my thoughts than your thoughts.*

Isaiah 55:9

The key to being receptive to God's will is surrender—and true surrender requires trust. A few years ago, I realized my lack of surrender was an outcome of not trusting God. Initially, I thought, "Of course I trust Him. I love Him!" Yet every time I take action without seeking His Word, when I'm tired of waiting, or when I don't like His answer and pursue my own way, I demonstrate that I don't trust that God's ways are better than my own.

It takes focused pursuit to maintain a healthy relationship with our Creator who, unlike the many distractions in my daily life, waits patiently rather than forcing Himself in and demanding my attention. It takes work, but when I take the time, it's always worth being sweetly reminded I am a daughter of the King.

Charisse McCumber
Senior Vice President & Shareholder at Holmes Murphy

He Knows Our Needs

*"Therefore I tell you, whatever you ask for in prayer,
believe that you have received it, and it will be yours."*

Mark 11:24

The Lord knows our needs before *we* even know we have a need. Awhile back, my husband was laid off. At that time, we had five children under eleven and no savings!

Before the layoff, the Holy Spirit had prompted me to pray every morning during our sons' naptime. So, when the news came, I was at peace.

A few months later, we started Garza Creative Group. The early years were a struggle. But within five years, we were an agency of record for several Fortune 500 companies and winning national awards.

Through persistent prayer, the Lord showed me my mission. From that point on, I hid His special word to me in my heart, assured that wherever I went He would go before me. And He has. He always makes a way—even when there doesn't seem to be a way.

Vicki Garza
CEO of Garza Creative

Natural Response

My son, give me your heart and let
your eyes delight in my ways.

Proverbs 23:26

*S*urrender is a humbling process for which not all people want to be first in line. Our struggles with surrender involve three things: experiences, disappointments, and fear.

You may not have enough personal history with God yet to know it's safe to leave things in His hands. Disappointment may have shattered your trust in others, the resulting hurt leaving you too fragile to give God a try to see if He will come through. Fear is a natural response to the unknown. When we let fear trample our faith and trust in God, we must rebuild the courage to not let those fears win.

Read Scriptures that confirm why God can be trusted. Let God remove what's hindering you from surrendering to Him and build up your faith. Then you can triumph in your trust in the Lord and overcome your fear of surrender.

Casseopia Dennis, MA

Know My Anxious Thoughts

Search me, God, and know my heart;
test me and know my anxious thoughts."

Psalm 139:23

Who am I? I've had to do a lot of work on this question. At one time, I had no idea who I was. I'd quit my corporate career to spend more time with my children. I failed at cooking, housekeeping, crafts, and even tennis. I really thought God had messed up when he made me … or maybe I just needed to try harder.

Am I alone in this loss of identity? I don't think so. I'm a work in progress. God has to continually remind me it's okay to not be like the women around me.

When self-doubt rears its head, remember: you are God's masterpiece. He has perfectly formed you for His plan for your life. Don't waste your time wondering who you are and wanting what others have. You're a perfect daughter of the King. Own it.

Lori Berry, MA-PC
Pastoral Counselor
4word Advisory Board Member

Go Another Way

For it is God's will that by doing good you should silence the ignorant talk of foolish people.

1 Peter 2:15

I've heard some people say that they don't do *anything* until they hear a word from God. And yet, Jesus' disciples didn't wait! We've all heard the principle: Something in motion stays in motion. The disciples lived this out. If something "seemed good," they'd do it, knowing that if they were not doing what God intended for them, He'd correct their path.

This practice is how women in the workplace can find success. Keep going and when you hit a roadblock, go another way. Don't change the end goal; change the direction you take to get there. If it's part of God's will for your life, you will find a way to achieve what you so ardently want to achieve. Ask Him to show you the way and resolve to follow where He leads.

Julie Ziglar Norman
Keynote Speaker, Author, Coach, and Daughter of Zig Ziglar

REFLECT & REFRESH

When have you pursued your own way instead of God's? Think of three steps you can take the next time the temptation to go your own way arises.

Do you know who you are? List five things you are in Christ, and commit them to memory.

Schedule time for prayer this week—whether an hour or five minutes. Ask God to remove anything that's hindering you from surrendering to Him.

Lord, thank you that before any other identity I carry, I am your daughter. Help me remember to seek your will for my life any time I'm tempted to forge my own path. When I'm unsure of who I am, help me see myself the way you do. When I don't know what to do, help me boldly take just one step, knowing you'll guide me as I pursue you. Don't let fear of going the wrong way keep me from moving. Instead help me trust you to lead me as I hold my own plans and dreams with an open hand.

Week 36

Embrace Today

Yes, my soul, find rest in God;
my hope comes from him.

Psalm 62:5

As a college graduate, about to enter the "real world," I wish I'd known how much God expected of me. I wish I'd made a lot more of my single years. I wish I'd embraced my life, instead of wishing it was something else.

In every stage of a woman's life, God's hand is on her. Every stage is strategic and important. God calls us to embrace today and say, "This is God's will for me. I need to make the most of it." When I look back, those single years were critical to what I'm doing now. Those were the years I started asking questions, and I've never stopped. Those struggles have been invaluable to me. I wouldn't be doing what I'm doing now if everything had just followed my script.

Carolyn Custis James
Author of *Half the Church: Recapturing God's Global Vision for Women* and *The Gospel of Ruth: Loving God Enough to Break the Rules*
4word Advisory Board Member

Solitary Pursuit

The Lord God had formed every beast ... and brought them to the man to see what he would call them. And whatever the man called every living creature, that was its name.

Genesis 2:19 ESV

*W*e were put on this earth to co-labor with God. In the garden of Eden, naming the zebra didn't stump God. He wanted to work with Adam!

As Ravi Zacharias said: "As we look at the difference between the secular world and the Christian world, here's what I concluded one day: In the secular world, they give you tiny, little meanings, with no ultimate meaning. They give you tiny, little purposes, with no ultimate purpose."[*]

When we don't follow God's direction, our life becomes just how fast we can check the list, get more followers, or climb to the top.

Don't forget. We are meant to work with God on something of great purpose to His plans.

Sandra Crawford Williamson
CEO of Crawford Creative Consulting
4word Advisory Board Member

---

[*] http://rzim.org/just-thinking-broadcasts/created-for-significance-part-3-of-4/

Change Course

He has made everything beautiful in its time.

Ecclesiastes 3:11

*Y*ou won't always have a choice, but if possible, try to tackle only one big change at a time. I waited to have kids until I felt a certain level of comfort in my job. I understood what was required and had established solid relationships with my boss and coworkers.

Many women worry that if they don't capitalize on opportunities for advancement, they'll be pigeonholed. That's a real risk, but it's one worth taking. Undertaking any big change in your personal life brings countless new challenges and adjustments. It's not impossible to do while you're starting a new job or role, but it's a lot harder.

Few career paths move forward in a straight line. If you hope to navigate successfully, start with a healthy, godly perspective on what work is (and is not), and then approach it with flexibility, humility, and courage.

Diane Paddison
Founder of 4word women
Former Executive Team at Trammell Crow Company,
CBRE, and ProLogis

Spiritual Food and Drink

Blessed are those who hunger
and thirst after righteousness.

Matthew 5:6 KJV

*H*ave you ever wondered what this passage means? Me too! A Bible scholar recently explained that we experience true happiness and inner joy as a result of an intense desire for the truth found only in the Scriptures. Jesus goes on to explain that hunger and thirst can only be temporarily quenched. One day of spending time in God's Word will sustain us for that day, but we need a daily diet of Bible study to thrive.

Plan for a daily intake of spiritual nourishment from His Word. Learn to live deliberately, and take control so that you have enough "spiritual food and drink" to maintain your spiritual health! It's a hard task in this busy world, but if we ask Him, God will help us find the time to nourish ourselves with what we hunger for most.

Constance Muecke Bawcom
Owner/CEO of VSL Lingerie

Proper Values

Do not throw away your confidence;
it will be richly rewarded. You need to persevere
so that when you have done the will of God,
you will receive what he has promised.

Hebrews 10:35–36

I come from a family of doers. My dad is a small business owner. I've always admired his honesty, integrity, and how he grew his business. Having grown up in that environment, I knew I could do anything I set my mind to.

People often tell me they wish they could make that leap into entrepreneurship, but it's not the right time. There's never a right time to take on something that big. If it's truly something you're passionate about, go for it. Like any big moment in life, it can be overwhelming if you look at it in its entirety. Turn to God and ask Him to give you perspective on your dream, whatever it is. If it's His will, you *will* find a way.

Amy Buchan Siegfried
Cofounder of Last Night's Game

REFLECT & REFRESH

Are you living like the "grass will be greener" in the next season? How can you invest in the place God has you today?

Do you believe God has called you to work with Him on a "great purpose"? Why or why not?

Have you had your daily intake of spiritual nourishment today? If not, find time for prayer and reading Scripture before the day ends.

Lord, thank you that I don't have to chase after the "tiny, little purposes" of this world. You've given me your great purpose. I'm grateful to partner with you in achieving that purpose in the world through my work. When I'm tempted to believe things will be better in the next season, remind me that I'm where I'm at for a reason. Give me eyes to see your way for my life as I navigate the twists and turns that will inevitably come my way in both my career and personal life. Help me to always put time with you first.

Week 37

Shine!

Then my soul will rejoice in the Lord
and delight in his salvation.

Psalm 35:9

*D*o you experience joy in your work? Unlike happiness, which is tied to external circumstances, joy flows from the inside out. Joy comes from knowing you're serving God to the best of your ability, using the gifts He's given you. You experience joy, and feel most alive, when you're living in alignment with God's plan for your life.

As you go about your day, consider yourself God's light in the marketplace. He's placed you in your role at this very time to make a difference in the lives of others. Even when you're having a tough day, or things seem to be falling apart, dig deep and find joy in God's divine plan.

Shine brightly as you juggle the tasks of your career, your family life, and your volunteer work, knowing that this season of life is part of His perfect plan for you. He created you to shine!

Susan Tolles
4word Regional Director of Local Groups, Central

Something to Give

Each of you should give what you have decided in your
heart to give, not reluctantly or under compulsion,
for God loves a cheerful giver.

2 Corinthians 9:7

I learned at an early age that we all have something to give or share with others. Some give money to those less fortunate. Others give time and coaching. Still others offer their talents and skills to someone else's project.

There are many ways to give, but one thing should remain the same. We should always give from our hearts— not out of obligation. When we give freely, we are showing the Christian way and leading by God's example. A cheerful heart will result! Try it. What is one thing you can do for someone in need today? Pay it forward.

Allison Jernigan
Vice President, Business Development, Cinemark Theatres

Present Yourself Well

"Love the Lord your God with all your heart
and with all your soul and with all your mind
and with all your strength."

Mark 12:29–30

*A*re you dealing with a "work bully"? If so, repeat this to yourself: "I'm God's. I'm working to serve Him."

Someone pushing you around at work might feel like a personal attack. But in most cases, workplace bullying isn't personal at all. "Bullying" is usually the result of misunderstanding. Most people believe the best way to deal with a bully is confrontation. However, there are times when it's wise to disengage.

Bullying can distract you from presenting yourself and Christ well in the workplace. Pray that God changes the situation, as well as the heart of your bully. In the end, there's nothing more important than loving and serving God, even if this means sacrificing your comfort, job, or the respect of your coworkers.

Diane Paddison
Founder of 4word women
Former Executive Team at Trammell Crow Company,
CBRE, and ProLogis

God Showing Up

"Arise, shine, for your light has come, and the glory of
the Lord rises upon you. See, darkness covers the earth
and thick darkness is over the peoples, but the Lord
rises upon you and his glory appears over you."

Isaiah 60:1–2

*H*ave you ever wished God would "show up" in a physical sense? Maybe you wanted to "prove" God is real
to someone. Maybe you needed a "burning bush" moment
yourself. If you've ever wished God would provide a sign,
you're not alone. In context, Isaiah 60:1–2 is a reminder
that the Redeemer will "show up" in His time. It's also a
call to let God's light shine in and through us.

We can be a "burning bush" for God that makes a big
difference for someone else. Invite the Lord to "show up"
in your life today and be a beacon for someone who needs
a reminder of (or introduction to) God's presence.

Commissioner Debi Bell
Territorial President of Women's Ministries, The Salvation Army,
USA Southern Territory

Live without Blinds

Let love be without hypocrisy.

Romans 12:9 NKJV

*A*s I drive through my neighborhood, I can see into my neighbors' living rooms. They have windows without blinds. I'm not trying to snoop, but they leave their lights on as if their homes are on display.

Christians are called to have lives without blinds. God desires to display our lives to draw people to Him. Jesus says, "Let your light shine before people so that they can see your good deeds and glorify your Father in heaven" (Matthew 5:16). Transparent lives that glorify God don't even have to be all good, just all *real*.

People need to see how God meets our needs in good times and bad. Real lives need real answers. Consider doing a little redecorating and taking down the blinds in your life. That way people can do a drive-by and peer into God's glory in your life.

Irrayna Uribe
Executive Director for Virtuous Communications, Inc.

REFLECT & REFRESH

Do you find joy in your work? How would seeing yourself as God's light in the marketplace change your attitude at work today?

What is one thing you can do today to "pay it forward" to someone in need?

Are you living a transparent life that reveals God's glory? Ask God how you can "take down the blinds" in your own life.

Lord, thank you that I have the opportunity to be your light in my workplace. When I am tempted to hide that light, give me courage to live my faith boldly so others can see and know you. Help me see my workplace as my mission field and give me your heart for my coworkers, even when I'm unfairly treated. Show up in my life today as I seek to pay forward all you have done for me.

Week 38

Balance Everything

There is a time for everything, and a season
for every activity under the heavens.

Ecclesiastes 3:1

When people hear my husband and I run a rapidly expanding business together, they often ask how we "balance everything." The truth is, we're not very balanced right now, and that's okay. We're accepting the crazy season we're in by doing what we can, as well as we can, together.

We all encounter seasons. Sometimes we can serve more at church or charities, as mentors, on boards, etc. Sometimes we don't have the time, or brain space, to take on additional responsibilities outside of family and work. We can't "should" on ourselves during seasons when we need to spend more time at work, with our spouse, or with our kids, or whatever. Don't say, "I *should* do this or that." Take Ecclesiastes 3 to heart. Trust there really is a season for all things. God understands and knows what he's doing—He'll use you in amazing ways, no matter what!

Heidi Rasmussen
Cofounder and COO, freshbenies

Right Role

The plans of the diligent lead to profit
as surely as haste leads to poverty.

Proverbs 21:5

*W*orking with your spouse is both a rewarding and a challenging experience. I was the founder and CEO of a technology company. In 2006, I asked my husband, Mark, who is a great salesperson, to join me and run sales for that business. We were not willing to sacrifice our relationship for the good of the business, so the keys to success were:

- Starting out with a high level of confidence in the probability of success.
- Staying in the right role in the right place, remembering I was not the boss at home.
- Communicating extensively.

Be professionals at work and be spouses at home.

In the end, our business goals were achieved and our marriage survived the challenge.

April Anthony
CEO of Homecare Homebase

Just Right

I press on toward the goal to win the prize for which
God has called me heavenward in Christ Jesus.

Philippians 3:14

God gave me just the right man—the one who would frustrate me to the point of giving up, only to reveal the work God was doing in me. God gave me the mirror of marriage to show me who I really am, so I couldn't keep denying I need to change. My husband's love for me is as imperfect as my love for him, but it is true.

God, keep teaching us forgiveness. You truly throw my ugly places to the bottom of the ocean and give me a new starting line every morning where you are beside me cheering me on. "Let's go!" you say, with an encouraging grin. Then you lean over and let me in on the secret. I'm going to win the race. There's a prize waiting for me at the end.

Lori Berry, MA-PC
Pastoral Counselor
4word Advisory Board Member

Believe the Best

Love bears all things, believes all things, hopes all things, endures all things.

1 Corinthians 13:7 ESV

Happy couples choose to believe the best about each other's intentions. When we're hurt, it's easy to allow ourselves to think, "He knew that would upset me and he said/did it anyway." Instead, let's choose to tell ourselves, "That hurt. He must not have realized it. I know he wouldn't intentionally hurt me." When we're hurt, the "easy" reaction is to stop believing in our spouse's love, but the vast majority of couples *do* care about each other, even in struggling marriages.

Believing the best about someone's intentions will make a significant difference in your life. Little changes of mind and attitude will even carry over into your workplace relationships. As followers of Jesus, if anyone has the ability to remain calm in the storm, it should be us.

Shaunti Feldhahn
Social Researcher
Best-selling Author of *For Women Only* and *The Surprising Secrets of Highly Happy Marriages*

Toxic Cycle

It's better to live alone in the corner of an attic than
with a quarrelsome wife in a lovely home.

Proverbs 21:9 NLT

Wife: What are you wearing to the party?

Hubby: My gray suit.

Wife: Has it been cleaned?

Hubby (long pause): ... and I signed us up to bring a dish.

Wife (sarcastically): Don't worry, *as usual,* the Secret Elf
will take care of it!

This conversation illustrates how the seed of resentment is planted and the habit of enabling begins. So how
do we stop this toxic cycle?

Pray about the situation. *Schedule* a time to talk with your
spouse. No one wants to be ambushed. *Share* how you are
feeling. *Ask* for what you want. Brainstorm *together* on ways
to improve. Agree on a *solution* to try. Give *feedback* in His
love language.

With careful communication and self-control, we can
learn to use our individual gifts to improve the team. After
all, God brought this partnership together for a reason.

Sandra Crawford Williamson
CEO of Crawford Creative Consulting
4word Advisory Board Member

REFLECT & REFRESH

Have you ever worked closely with a spouse or a friend? How did you maintain healthy roles and communication?

Is there anything you need to ask for forgiveness for from your spouse, child, or a friend? Ask God for the humility and courage to both ask for and extend forgiveness today.

Do you need to believe the best about someone's intentions today?

Lord, thank you for my spouse, my children, my friends, and my coworkers who point me to you. Teach me to put my relationships above all else, first with you and then with my family. When my priorities are askew, show me how to realign them and get back on track. Help me to be humble and ask for forgiveness when I'm in the wrong, and help me be quick to forgive others. Thank you for setting the example of forgiveness by forgiving me when I fall short. I want to be a woman who stays calm in the storm, because I am founded on the rock of your love.

Week 39

Give Him the Reins

A bruised reed he will not break,
and a smoldering wick he will not snuff out,
till he has brought justice through to victory.

Matthew 12:20

*H*ave you ever noticed that regardless of what size purse you're carrying it's always full? We tend to make use of what we're given. The same goes for work: if we allow it to take up our whole day, it will. But if we set firm boundaries, we'll be surprised at what we accomplish in a shorter amount of time.

Accept that others may not share your boundaries around work. You can't control how they respond. You can and should impose limits in a respectful way.

No one gets this right all the time. I'm committed to do the best I can, learning and making adjustments as I go along, and trusting that God is working in it all. Give God the reins of your workload and see where He guides.

Diane Paddison
Founder of 4word women
Former Executive Team at Trammell Crow Company,
CBRE, and ProLogis

Come to Grips

I will refresh the weary and satisfy the faint.

Jeremiah 31:25

We can be physically at rest, yet experience utter turmoil on the inside. We may be sitting on a couch, yet our emotions are driving us to crippling anxiety, sadness, or even despair. True rest and peace start with the heart. They're inside jobs.

Not long ago, we almost lost my mom to an aortic dissection. It's a miracle she's alive and healthy today. In those dark hours of not knowing if she'd live or die, our circumstances were certainly not promoting peace and rest. In the midst of tidal waves of emotion, we prayed. His peace and presence carried us!

How do we find this rest and peace? Come to grips with the reality that we cannot produce either one! Only God can give us true rest and peace. When we seek Him with all of our heart, rest and peace will find us.

Susan Thomas
Licensed Professional Counselor
Senior Pastor's Wife, Keystone Church

Set a Good Rhythm

The fear of the Lord leads to life; then one rests content,
untouched by trouble.

Proverbs 19:23

*O*ur bodies produce a limited amount of cortisol each day. Cortisol enables us to wake up, think, complete tasks, and function. However, what comes up must come down. Once the cortisol is used, our body goes through a depletion period. Yet most of us continue to push ourselves. We burn out by ignoring our natural and spiritual rhythms.

Early in my career, I was accustomed to burning the oil at both ends. Experiencing burnout showed me how much I'd been striving in my own effort, instead of trusting the Lord. Truly resting requires truly trusting. Rest is when I place my faith in God, instead of in myself. I've learned to create margin, resting strategically in the Lord's presence, to honor the ebb and flow of my natural and spiritual rhythms. Set a good rhythm for today and place your faith in Him.

Shannan Crawford, PsyD
Licensed Psychologist
CEO Dr. Crawford & Associates, PLLC

Set the Pace

Zaccheus was trying to see who Jesus was,
and was unable because of the crowd, for he was
small in stature. So he ran on ahead and climbed up
into a sycamore tree in order to see Him.

Luke 19:3-4 NASB

*I*n our culture, we're always running toward something—status, visible success, even the idea of a busy calendar. What would happen if we reconsidered our direction? What if, like Zaccheus, we ran toward Jesus?

My Young Life leader shared this visual with me: Suppose you're standing at the start of a race, facing the finish line. Would rotating a couple degrees to the left or the right make a difference? Probably not in the beginning, but miles down the trail you'd be completely off track. That one or two degree shift in the beginning would change the entire outcome of the run.

Be sure you're running ahead of the crowd—in the right direction. Run toward Jesus with precision.

Lauren Ford
Young Life Capernaum Director

Running on Fumes

He is not served by human hands, as if he needed anything, because he himself gives all people life and breath and everything else.

Acts 17:25

*A*re you stressed out, running on fumes, snapping at everybody, always tired? I know people who seem to keep their head in all situations. I want that! Often, though, I'm running, running, running ... but never feeling like I'm getting anywhere.

I hold my breath all the time. I put my head down, power through, and strive, instead of deciding to just breathe. I grab control and hold tight to my plans, instead of resting in the peace that comes with knowing God is doing this thing, not me.

God doesn't actually need me to accomplish His purposes. God works *in* me and *through* me. God lets me grow by serving Him. It's *His* power, not mine, that gets me through each day. It's up to me to rest in God's promises and give Him control.

Lori Berry, MA-PC
Pastoral Counselor
4word Advisory Board Member

REFLECT & REFRESH

Are there any boundaries you need to put up around your work schedule to protect what is important to you? Be specific.

Do you believe that God's power, not your own, is sufficient to get you through the day? Why or why not?

Do you struggle with burnout? How can you build times of rest into your week?

Lord, thank you that my worth is not dependent on how much I accomplish or how many accolades I acquire. I believe that my worth is in you alone, giving me permission to stop and rest in you. Teach me to not just rest, but rest well in a way that honors you. By taking time to rest, I know I am admitting that I can't do everything. Instead, I'm trusting you to take care of me. Show me what new boundaries I need to build. Give me the strength to say "no" when my schedule gets too full. Thank you that I can do all things through your strength, not my own.

Week 40

Pulse Check

You make known to me the path of life;
in your presence there is fullness of joy.

Psalm 16:11 ESV

My husband and I do frequent marriage pulse checks. We ask each other how we're doing. Then we ask, "Okay, but how are *you* really doing?" It's marriage first, then children, then work, with God saturating the equation.

If you're struggling with this balancing act, hold fast to what's most important: your heavenly Father, who loves you more than you love your own children. He'll guide you down the right path. It may not be the most glamorous, or bring the most money or accolades, but you cannot put a price on the peace that surpasses understanding when you're smack in the center of His will.

Seek God over your husband, your children, your career, and your friends. Everything else will align, and you'll find that He is more than enough.

Rebecca Carrell
"Mornings with Jeff & Rebecca," 90.9 KCBI
Author, Bible Teacher, Conference Speaker

Power of Prayer

*"If you remain in me and my words remain in you,
ask whatever you wish, and it will be done for you."*

John 15:7

I believe in the power of prayer. Sometimes you might be led to stay in a company, because you can be a force of change. Even if you aren't in a position of power to cause change, you can still pray and watch for signs of change within the company and leadership. Just remember, change takes time. If God has placed it on your heart to implement a change in your workplace, it's for a reason. He *will* supply you with the wisdom and perseverance to see the change through to the end—or He'll use you to inspire the person who will ultimately make the change.

Pray for those who aren't in a position to change big things, and pray for those who are. Find other colleagues willing to join your prayer efforts and, together, lift up your workplace.

Lisbeth McNabb
Digital Executive
4word Board Member

Inability to Manage

Keep your lives free from the love of money
and be content with what you have.

Hebrews 13:5

*M*ost women who are struggling with finding balance suffer from what I call "Super Woman Syndrome." It's a woman's nature to want to prove she's capable of doing it all. By doing it all, she's less likely to let anyone down ... including God. However, she ends up letting herself down instead. This can only go on for so long before she hits a breaking point.

Making oneself a priority is of core importance. Typically, when I ask women what they are doing for themselves, they don't have an answer.

Often, it's not the inability to manage work and life that's the problem. Rather, women are not making their self-contentment a priority, or even including it in the equation. In essence, they've lost themselves and forgotten who they are.

As His child, God wants you to see your worth, as He sees it.

Fabi Howard, MA, LPC
Speaker & Professional Coach at Living StrongHer

How Do You Define Success?

Let not steadfast love and faithfulness forsake you;
bind them around your neck; write them on the tablet
of your heart. So you will find favor and good success.

Proverbs 3:3–4 ESV

When I speak at writers conferences, the question attendees seem most interested in having answered is, "How can I be successful?" My answer? "That depends on your definition of success." For some, success simply means being published. For others, it means writing a best-selling novel that will bankroll their writer's mansion by the sea.

So how does God define success? In Matthew 22:36–40, Jesus explains that by loving God and loving others we fulfill all of God's commandments. In other words, it's not so much what I do, but who I am as I do it that matters. As we climb the ladder of success, may our priority be to love those climbing alongside us well, instead of focusing on how high we can climb.

Vicki J. Kuyper
Speaker, Author, and Freelance Writer

Perfect Intentionality

My frame was not hidden from you when
I was made in the secret place, when I was
woven together in the depths of the earth.

Psalm 139:15

Trusting God with how He gifted me has been a long process. Even at age twelve, I remember struggling with a tension between the roles I saw women fill in our conservative Christian church and how I was wired. I didn't fit the traditional mold for women, but I didn't know how to talk with God about it.

This tension became a place of quiet sorrow and shame. By studying the Hebrew words used in Psalm 139, I realized God intentionally formed me exactly the way He wanted. I'm not too much, nor am I not enough, of the "best" kind of Christian woman. My path didn't instantly become smooth once I realized this truth. But it's helped me grow in my trust of a good God who guides me in His perfect intentionality.

Andrea Nelson Trice
Senior Fellow, Sagamore Institute

REFLECT & REFRESH

Are there areas of your life that need some "priority attention"?

Do you suffer from "Super Woman Syndrome"? What steps can you take to invest in your own well-being this week?

Take a few minutes to read Psalm 139. How would believing that God "intentionally formed your essence" change how you view yourself and how you spend your time?

Lord, forgive me when I fall victim to "Super Woman Syndrome" and believe the lie that I have to do everything I can to keep the trains running on time. I believe that you are in control, but too often I fail to put time with you first, because my to-do list is too long. May the strengths and gifts you have given me be my source of worth, instead of my ability to perform. Teach me to take care of myself as I take care of others and help me know when to readjust my priorities. Thank you for creating me uniquely, just as I am.

Week 41

Who Is Jesus?

"John was a lamp that burned and gave light,
and you chose for a time to enjoy his light.
I have testimony weightier than that of John."

John 5:35–36

It all started with my role as Mary in the Christmas nativity. I took the assignment very seriously. When a shepherd reached out to touch baby Jesus, I shouted, "Mrs. Byron! Somebody's touching the baby!" Not on my watch.

I was blessed with an early love of liturgy and the Catholic rituals. I was content. Then one day, all of that beauty dialed up into Technicolor as I saw someone I thought I knew in a completely different light. I saw Jesus as my everything and not just a figure on the cross. I got to know this Jesus for whom all the beautiful liturgy was created. Now, the brightness of liturgy is amplified by the burning and shining lamp that emanates from my core. Who is Jesus to you?

Sandy Swider
Leadership Coach and Managing Director, 4word Local Groups

A Way Out

No temptation has overtaken you except
what is common to mankind. And God is faithful;
he will not let you be tempted beyond what you
can bear. But when you are tempted, he will
also provide a way out so that you can endure it.

1 Corinthians 10:13

*D*on't minimize. Don't justify. Run!

I'm still a sinner and the enemy has not taken a break from tempting me. As sinners, we tend to minimize our sins when we want to do or say something. Wondering if you're minimizing something? Bring it to the light. Compare it to God's Word, pray about it, confess it to God, talk about it with a wise friend or accountability partner.

We all have a voice that starts warning us when we're entering a sinful situation. The problem is most of us ignore these signals. One way to right your situation is to run from sin. Go in a different direction. Pray for God to show you a way out.

Ines Franklin
Chapel Pastor at Mariners Church

Tranquility

Dear friends, now we are children of God, and what we will be has not yet been made known.

1 John 3:2

The most precious gift Dan and I have received from God is the tranquility that came from understanding our calling as adoptive parents. Those early years with our two sons were exhausting, and even frightening. Many times we asked, "Are you sure, God? Certainly you chose someone else and we jumped in the way!" Yet, we knew. This was indeed our gift.

There are many varieties of successful couples and families. God is at work in all of us. Dan and I have been open about our adoption experience, wanting to assure others that, with God's help, they may also be up to the challenge of salvaging the lives of abused and neglected children. Imagine receiving the gift of contentment, knowing your life's purpose! If you keep yourself open to God, you too can receive this gift of clarity regarding His will for your family.

Sonja Wilson
Principal, Strategy2Funding
4word Tulsa Local Group Leader

Harmless

Respect everyone, and love the family of believers.

1 Peter 2:17 NLT

*W*hen men and women work together in close quarters, flirting is bound to happen. Many people consider it "harmless." Others openly advocate flirting to get what you want. But flirting at work is rarely harmless. It's a bad idea, even if both people are single and enjoy the interaction.

To avoid being perceived as flirtatious, I've seen some women adopt a coldly impersonal attitude. This approach is counterproductive, because it often alienates people. As Christians, we're ambassadors of God. Opening our hearts to, and caring about, the people we work with is one of the primary ways we can "be like Christ" at work. It's actually good for business too.

We all want to believe our "innocent flirtation" could never lead anywhere regrettable. But flirting can go wrong in so many ways. It's easier to say no to flirting than to correct a bigger problem down the line.

Diane Paddison
Founder of 4word women
Former Executive Team at Trammell Crow Company,
CBRE, and ProLogis

Cross the Road

"Which of these three do you think was a neighbor to
the man who fell into the hands of robbers?" The expert
in the law replied, "The one who had mercy on him."
Jesus told him, "Go and do likewise."

Luke 10:36–37

*W*hy do I think my neighbor is only someone who looks like me? Someone who isn't too dirty, too "damaged," too beat up or beat down? Someone who lives on my side of the street? It's so much easier, so much neater, so much simpler, to pass by the neighbors I don't know, don't understand, and who don't resemble me.

Jesus asks me to cross the street—and cross the world—to get up close enough to hear their heartbeat, to really see the neighbor who is truly different from me. He asks me to love them, show mercy on them, share with them some of the blessings He's given me. May the Lord help me have the Samaritan's vision, heart, and courage.

Patricia Myers
Former Director, Talent Management
Director, Leadership Development for National Commercial
Bank of Saudi Arabia (NCB)
Executive Coach and 4word Board Member

REFLECT & REFRESH

Is there a weakness, temptation, or outright sin you need to run away from?

Are you more likely to "flirt innocently" at work or act coldly toward those of the opposite sex? How can you adopt a Christlike attitude toward the opposite sex at work?

Who is Jesus to you?

Lord, thank you that there is no temptation I cannot stand against, because you are with me. Reveal any areas of weakness in my life that could lead to sin, and if I am living in sin against you, I repent of my sin and ask you to help me live in the freedom of your forgiveness. I want to love my neighbor as I have been loved by you—help me to "cross the street" to see and love them, especially when they don't look like me. I want to be your hands and feet in my workplace.

Week 42

Lights for Christ

You were once darkness, but now you are light
in the Lord. Walk as children of light.

Ephesians 5:8 NKJV

This verse reminds me of those who were a light to me before I was born again in my midtwenties.

There was my godly grandmother, known for her commitment, faithfulness, and service to others. In college, there was a girl in my dorm who was always happy, smiling, and singing! I wanted to be like her, even though I never knew her name. When I worked for the founder of Mary Kay Cosmetics, she lived her faith. I always "researched" what I felt would be important to my job, so I began reading books about Christianity. When I came to Christ, it felt like coming home.

Think about the "lights" for Christ who have touched your life. Some may not even realize the impact they made. As we shine, we never know who's watching—and who may, one day, look back with thankfulness on our testimony.

Jennifer Cook
Foundation and Museum Director, Mary Kay Inc.

Little Christ

*Therefore let us stop passing judgment on one another.
Instead, make up your mind not to put any stumbling
block or obstacle in the way of a brother or sister.*

Romans 14:13

*M*edia research tells us that in today's culture it takes seconds for us to make a judgment.* As a media producer and consultant, I educate clients on how to grab attention fast, especially on social media platforms. Pictures and words matter. The downside is that we've become an overly critical culture. Today on social media, people can get vicious.

As Christians, we need to be extra cautious. Just because we're armed with God's truth doesn't give us the authority to be rude. Humor and sarcasm can produce laughs, but they can also backfire, causing spiritual walls. Negative perceptions can quickly be formed about Christianity, and more importantly, about God's nature.

Christian means "little Christ." Are you a "little Christ" when posting? Let's get the culture's attention by being known for reflecting God's grace and mercy.

Kathleen Cooke
Cofounder Cooke Pictures and The Influence Lab
4word Advisory Board Member

---

* https://en.wikipedia.org/wiki/Thin-slicing

Glorify Your Father

Not to us, O Lord, not to us,
but to your name give glory.

Psalm 115:1 ESV

*A*s an anesthesiologist, I often found it challenging to guide conversations toward spiritual matters, so it was nice when my break coincided with one of my nurses, who'd been a missionary in Asia. During one of our chats, another nurse joined in, sharing that she'd once been a Sunday school teacher. I knew her life had become a mess and prayed for an opportunity to speak with her. It didn't come, as she soon resigned.

Weeks later, that same nurse called me at home. Shocked, I thought God had given me another chance! I quickly tried to recall the points I needed to share, but the conversation was brief. She told me she'd seen how I had lived my life—and was rededicating her life to the Lord. That was it. The workplace may not be conducive to conversations of faith, but it is conducive to living your faith.

Susan B. Smalling, MD
4word: Austin Board

Fight Your Tendency

Here we have no lasting city,
but we seek the city that is to come.

Hebrews 13:14 ESV

*I*f you're considering a career change (or leaving your career behind altogether) the first step is obvious—pray. Pray that you're not making this decision in the middle of crisis (I'm tired, I'm angry with my boss, I've failed so I want to run away . . .). Look for confirmation in Scripture, through the Holy Spirit, and through the advice of godly friends and mentors.

Most women who talk to me about quitting their jobs are moms. Their health, sanity, and relationship with their family is suffering. When I talk to single women, they're trying to reconcile fulfilling their calling with doing something that just pays the bills. Many also wonder if they're going to meet a future mate as they pursue their career.

Remember, God desires to be in a relationship with us. We must fight our tendency to try to do everything on our own.

Sonya Crawford Bearson
Former Broadcast Journalist and Current Stay-at-Home Mother

Catalyst

*And we urge you, brothers and sisters, warn those
who are idle and disruptive, encourage the
disheartened, help the weak, be patient with everyone.*

1 Thessalonians 5:14

Has God ever used someone to drastically change your life?

One woman who unknowingly helped me as a newly divorced mother of two toddlers is contemporary Christian singer Amy Grant. I listened to her song, "El Shaddai," nearly every day during the painful season of my divorce.

Little did I know that fifteen years later, I would sit across the table from Amy and get to share how deeply she impacted my life. It was a precious few hours of talking and praying together that I will never forget.

God uses His followers to deeply impact the lives of others. Sometimes we're a catalyst for a significant change in someone's life, whether we know it at the time or not. Who can you be a catalyst for today?

Diane Paddison
Founder of 4word women
Former Executive Team at Trammell Crow Company,
CBRE, and ProLogis

REFLECT & REFRESH

Does your social media activity reflect who you are as a "little Christ"?

Are you sharing your faith through your actions at work? What step could you take to live out your faith in the workplace this week?

Ask God to use you as a catalyst for positive change in the lives of your coworkers.

Lord, thank you for the testimonies of those who have pointed me toward you. I too want to be a catalyst for others to seek, find and know you as their Savior. Show me how I can share my faith in you not just with words, but in my actions and through the way I treat others. I want to represent you well, including on social media. Reveal the areas of my life where I am not acting as a "little Christ," so I can make the changes necessary to reflect your grace and mercy in all that I do. Use my life to reveal your glory and lead those around me to you.

Week 43

Lengthen Your Stride

> Don't you realize that in a race everyone runs, but only
> one person gets the prize? So run to win!
>
> *1 Corinthians 9:24 NLT*

*M*y dear friend and mentor Norma, loves to remind me that "life is a marathon, not a sprint."

How right she is! When I started 4word, I transitioned my successful full-time career to working part-time. At fifty-five, I moved out of the day-to-day corporate world altogether to focus full-time on nonprofit and corporate board work. The shape of my career continues to change and develop. And as Norma would say, I still have a long way to go!

With its constant flow of demands and deadlines, work often feels like a sprint, but it doesn't have to be one. Sprinters are fast, but they don't get very far. If you want your career to go places, you need to slow your pace, lengthen your stride, and take deep breaths.

Diane Paddison
Founder of 4word women
Former Executive Team at Trammell Crow Company,
CBRE, and ProLogis

Our Gain

What do workers gain from their toil?
I know that there is nothing better for people
than to be happy and to do good while they live.
That each of them may eat and drink, and find
satisfaction in all their toil—this is the gift of God.

Ecclesiastes 3:9, 12–13

*D*o you ever read the notes in your study Bible? The comments for Ecclesiastes 3:9–13 seem so applicable for those struggling in the workplace. In my study Bible, the notes say, "Your ability to enjoy your work depends to a large extent upon your attitude. Work becomes toil when you lose the sense of purpose that God intended for it. We can enjoy our work if we remember that God has equipped us for particular tasks and realize that the fruit of our labor is a gift from Him."[*]

Now's the perfect time to remind yourself of these truths, take a deep breath, and refocus. The Lord has hand-picked you to be right where you are for His purposes.

Constance Muecke Bawcom
Owner/CEO of VSL Lingerie

---

[*] Life Application Bible, The Living Bible (Wheaton, IL: Tyndale House Publishers and Youth For Christ/USA, 1988).

He Provides

"You do not even know what will happen tomorrow.
What is your life? You are a mist that appears
for a little while and then vanishes."

James 4:14

*I*f God is calling you to do something, even if it seems as crazy as walking on water, step out in faith!

Waves may still crash around you, the wind might blow, and there may be moments where you think you'll drown. But based on my life experiences—leaving the military to become a missionary in the midst of the stock market crash, starting my own business on the heels of my marriage crumbling and not having any income, taking a year off to travel the globe, then moving to Dallas on faith with no job and only a dream of living out my passion to be a speaker and "visionary world changer"—let me just say: God provides! Getting out of the boat is the only way we get to experience the thrill of walking on water. It's so worth it!

Rachel Sherburne
Speaker and Strategic Coach
4word Regional Director, Local Groups, West

Our Counselor

You guide me with your counsel.

Psalm 73:24

*I*sn't it comforting to know we have a Counselor we don't have to call, schedule an appointment, or pay? God is so close, and He's dying to speak to you! He wants to hear what's on our heart and speak love and truth to you. Sometimes, that takes place through His Word, sometimes it's through the inner workings of our heart. Regardless, He's got your back and your right hand.

I picture a dad holding his daughter's hand, walking beside her, protecting her, and delighting in her. What I love about Psalm 73 is that it goes on to explain that even when I fall short, which is pretty much every day, God doesn't go anywhere. He's not ashamed of my sin. He doesn't even see it. So go to Him, go to your Daddy and ask for His will and guidance. Give Him the desires of your heart, and He'll respond.

Kaitlin Murphy Arduino
Executive Vice President of Murphy Development Company

Token Woman

God's gifts and his call are irrevocable.

Romans 11:29

No one wants to be the "token" woman at work. During my twenty years in private practice, I got into the habit of striving to be gender-neutral. Given the lack of women in leadership at large law firms, I figured I'd have to downplay my motherhood to get ahead.

Then, one day, I was presenting my qualifications to a new client and asked, "What are you looking for in a lawyer?"

He replied, "I'd really like a woman to handle this matter."

His comment challenged my thinking. I've come to realize that gender is part of my God-given identity. It's part of my calling at home and at work.

Have you ever considered your gender as part of your God-given work? If not, start today! At the foundation of God's plan for you is the fact that you're a woman. Embrace that fact and live in the fullness of His will for your life!

Susan DiMickele
SVP & General Counsel, National Church Residences

REFLECT & REFRESH

Are you sprinting too fast at work? What steps can you take to "slow your pace, lengthen your stride, and take a deep breath"?

Do you enjoy your work? How would seeing your work as a way to serve God change how you feel about your job?

Do you find yourself striving to be "gender neutral" at work? How could being a woman enhance your identity and add to your strengths in the workplace?

Lord, thank you that you have created me to work, partnering with you to bring your kingdom here on earth. Thank you for the joy that I can find in my work when I'm aligned with your purpose. When you call me to take a leap, give me the courage to jump out of the boat and trust your provision. When I'm sprinting too fast, give me the courage to slow my pace and lengthen my stride. I want to reach the finish line and hear you say "well done."

Week 44

Heart's Desire

Now to him who is able to do immeasurably more
than all we ask or imagine, according to his power
that is at work within us, to him be glory in the church
and in Christ Jesus throughout all generations,
for ever and ever! Amen.

Ephesians 3:20–21

*A*s an eleven-year-old, I toured the White House. I was
the president of my school at the time and had such
great admiration for President Ronald Reagan that I wrote
a letter "from one president to another." Ha!

The Lord knew my desires as a little girl—in fact, I
believe He put those desires in my heart. Years later, as
I walked through the gates of the White House to report
to work, I was awed by His "immeasurably more than we
ask or imagine" in my life. The six jobs I had at the White
House were not without challenge, but the Lord continually surprised me with His goodness.

Charity Wallace
Founder & Principal at Wallace Global Impact
Senior Advisor at the George W. Bush Institute
4word Advisory Board Member

Peculiar Possession

But you are a chosen people, a royal priesthood,
a holy nation, God's special possession, that you
may declare the praises of him who called you
out of darkness into his wonderful light.

1 Peter 2:9

*W*ould you consider yourself "peculiar" or a possession of God? We're each born with unique and distinctive qualities. Through each season of life, we learn new ways to use these qualities to help benefit our family, earn a living at work, and support the community in which we live.

I've learned my unique qualities are leadership, prayer, and encouragement. As a small business owner, author, wife, mother, and "nana," God has used my talents in ways I never planned or imagined. I thought all my previous achievements were my destination in life, but they were simply stepping stones leading toward the path of author and speaker.

Learning to trust God creates endless possibilities. Embrace your identity and identify your distinct qualities! *You* are a "peculiar" person. Value your identity!

Rhonda B. Gaines
Founder/CEO of RBG Business Solutions, LLC

Reason to Say No

We have different gifts,
according to the grace given to each of us.

Romans 12:6

*T*he guilt that comes with motherhood can be overwhelming. Working mothers feel guilty because it can look like we're choosing work over our kids. We buy store-bought cupcakes, instead of baking a Pinterest masterpiece.

Full time stay-at-home moms feel guilty, believing they have no reason to say no. They feel the pressure to be the room mom, carpool volunteer, and bring snacks for soccer.

Whatever your calling looks like, you should *never* feel inadequate in your position. Claim these three truths: 1) You are uniquely gifted (Romans 12:4–8), 2) God answers prayer—and sometimes the answer is a protective no (1 John 5:14–15), 3) God can provide the strength for this situation (Isaiah 40:31).

We're all in this together. Remember that grace, love, and support are what we need in abundance as we discover God's call in our life.

Sandra Crawford Williamson
CEO of Crawford Creative Consulting
4word Advisory Board Member

Worthy Co-Laborer

We keep on praying for you, asking our God
to enable you to live a life worthy of his call.
May he give you the power to accomplish all the
good things your faith prompts you to do.

2 Thessalonians 1:11 NLT

*I*t's a priority to listen for God's call in all dimensions of our lives, so we can glorify Him, bless our neighbors, and find purpose and soul satisfaction. That doesn't always translate into getting our "dream job" or a promotion. Often our calling includes sacrifice and suffering.

It's important for women to understand that the world's institutions and workplaces need them. God intended for our world to be stewarded and shepherded by women and men alike, beginning with Adam and Eve, who together bore the image of God.

Ask God to make you a worthy co-laborer and to bless your calling with favor and clear direction as you arrive to work every day.

Katelyn Beaty
Author of *A Woman's Place*
Editor at Large of *Christianity Today* magazine

Draw the Line

Moreover, it is required of stewards
that they be found faithful.

1 Corinthians 4:2 ESV

Many women are drawn toward helping others. That's not a bad thing. As Christians in the work force, part of our calling is to serve and minister to those around us. But serving beyond our capacity can take a mental and emotional toll, leading to exhaustion, bitterness, and burn out.

My gifts and my passions lead me toward mentoring, which I do in addition to my job. But I don't volunteer to take notes in meetings, because note taking interferes with my ability to think critically during discussions. There are a multitude of things I don't do, in order to be available for the things God has called me to do.

Are you serving beyond your capacity? Today, draw the line. Make a commitment (to yourself and others) to start being a good steward of your time and talents.

Diane Paddison
Founder of 4word women
Former Executive Team at Trammell Crow Company,
CBRE, and ProLogis

REFLECT & REFRESH

Do you believe God? How could believing that God wants to do "immeasurably more than all we ask or imagine" impact your life?

In what areas of your life are you not currently trusting God?

Do you see yourself as a co-laborer with Christ? Reflect on what that means to you and your work.

> Lord, thank you for your promise that you will do "immeasurably more than all we ask or imagine" in my life. I praise you for the times you have blown my hopes and expectations out of the water. Help me to not just believe in you, but to truly believe you and your promises. Show me where I am not fully trusting you and help me surrender my whole life—my work, my family, my hopes, and my dreams—to you. I am so thankful to be chosen as a co-laborer with you, partnering to bring your kingdom to those around me.

Week 45

Perfectly Unique

Those who trust in themselves are fools,
but those who walk in wisdom are kept safe.

Proverbs 28:26

*A*s a manager, it's not enough to be good at getting your own work done. You have to take a lot of other people into account. It can be exciting to try to figure people out and invigorating to help them reach their goals. It can also be draining to motivate a disengaged employee or frustrating to see someone's mistakes or bad attitude dragging your whole team down.

As a manager, you're uniquely able to impact the lives of those who report to you. This power is a gift. Like all gifts, you should approach it from the perspective of God's grace.

Managing other people is hard work, and isn't always comfortable. But despite its challenges, management is an opportunity to impact someone's life and be a powerful beacon of Christ in the workplace.

Diane Paddison
Founder of 4word women
Former Executive Team at Trammell Crow Company,
CBRE, and ProLogis

Abiding

I consider my life worth nothing to me;
my only aim is to finish the race and complete the
task the Lord Jesus has given me—the task of
testifying to the good news of God's grace.

Acts 20:24

I was pursuing the pictures I'd created in my head of what I believed my life was going to look like, instead of God's will for my life. In 2008, all of that changed when I almost lost my life. Eight difficult months of recovery actually refreshed my spirit. It was time for me to fully submit to the Lord's will. My time of recovery really made me press into the Lord, listen, read His Word, and write down everything I heard and learned.

If you're struggling to determine what God's will is for you, seek Him in a new way. Start by just saying yes to Him, no matter what. It's a scary step, but when we're totally in, He can take us on His journey.

Shari Rigby
Actress, Writer, Director, and Speaker

Works of Art

We are God's handiwork, created in Christ Jesus
to do good works, which God prepared
in advance for us to do.

Ephesians 2:10

I'm craft challenged. If someone sends me a DIY from Pinterest, I figure out how to buy it. Handcrafting anything seems like a ton of work to me.

Reflecting on the word *handiwork* makes me consider the level of care God took in creating me. He planned in advance for us. That's how special we are to Him.

I feel a sense of urgency and excitement about being "created in Christ Jesus to do good works." He's uniquely gifted me, and I want to find out what that means. I have a purpose and I want to be diligent.

In what ways am I using my God-given abilities to bring Him glory? What does He want me to be doing? We are all "works of art" created to extend the blessing that God has given to us to the world.

Sandra Crawford Williamson
CEO of Crawford Creative Consulting
4word Advisory Board Member

Timing Is Everything

My times are in your hands.

Psalm 31:15

*W*e hear it throughout life: Timing is everything. But when God is taken out of the concept of timing, there's nothing left to do but to try and figure out how we—with all of our human limitations—are going to figure out how to do things. Timing without God will always result in us feeling small, scared, and insecure.

God knows the end at the beginning. Only God can understand and control the timing of life's events. Only He can provide us with the peace to stand joyfully and confidently, while we wait for His timing to reveal itself to us. His timing is incredible, and we are incredible in it. My prayer is that we can step boldly into the next season of our lives fully experiencing the purposes for which He has sent us into the world, into our communities, and even into our families. I see change coming, and it's about time.

Cynthia Garrett
TV Host, Author, Motivational Speaker, and Evangelist

Free from Guilt

Like a city whose walls are broken through
is a person who lacks self-control.

Proverbs 25:28

*Y*ou and I are busy woman. We tackle roles of businesswoman, fashion designer, hair stylist, chef, vet, plumber, and chauffeur—all before 7:30 a.m.

One day during my Quiet Time, the Lord used the verse above to free me from guilt. The Lord showed me a city overrun by enemies, villagers running amok. Envision a disturbed ant hill in utter chaos. When walls are broken down, everything can get in. With this in mind, I reflected on my life, my schedule, and my "busy-ness."

Sometimes, I say yes yet secretly wish I'd said no. The Lord has shown me that self-control is my right and my duty to protect my city from being besieged. When I say no, I claim freedom from guilt and set healthy boundaries.

Today, declare freedom in your life from feeling besieged—and let go of any guilt.

Dr. Brooke Jones
Founder & CEO of Stronger than Espresso

REFLECT & REFRESH

*Are you struggling to determine God's will for your life?
Write down three steps you can take to abide in Him this
week as you seek His will.*

*Take some time to reflect on the ways you are using
your God-given abilities to bring Him glory.*

*How can you show God's grace to those you manage at
work this week?*

Lord, thank you for your perfect timing. I often
forget that I am not the one in control of the timing of my days. Give me patience as I trust you to
reveal your plan to me at the right time and not
one moment too early or too late. I believe you
have given me unique gifts and a purpose that
glorifies you. Help me remember that I am a work
of art, created by you on purpose. I want to step
boldly into the next season of my life and fully
experience your purpose for me.

Week 46

Great Courage

Immediately the rooster crowed the second time.
Then Peter remembered the word Jesus had spoken
to him: "Before the rooster crows twice you will disown
me three times." And he broke down and wept.

Mark 14:72

*A*t the 2017 Oscar Awards ceremony, viewers witnessed a mistake in the announcement of the winner of the Best Movie Award. We can imagine the feelings of the two accountants who ultimately lost their jobs. Dashing out onto the stage to declare a mistake had been made required great courage.

God has the plan for our lives, a plan not dependent on our perfection. Taking responsibility for our mistakes and failures, including doing the right thing, is part of our walk as a follower of Christ. To do so requires courage and faith that God will not let our mistakes thwart His good plans for us.

Kim King
Author of *When Women Give*
Former Chief Attorney of Compliance
at ExxonMobil Corporation

Hurt Unwasted

"For if you forgive other people when they sin
against you, your heavenly Father will also forgive you."

Matthew 6:14-15

*A*t the age of six, my daughter Ashlyn was sexually violated by a man who was close to our family. It's amazing how God began working on Ashlyn's heart to forgive her violator before I could even think about considering the option of forgiveness. Ashlyn now shares her story with others as she feels called to do so and it continues to bring so much healing to her. God is so good!

As a parent, it's hard to make sense of something like this happening to your precious baby. While I don't believe God meant for this to happen, I truly believe He knew we would do something about it. What someone else meant for evil, God is using for good.

God doesn't waste pain. Share your story with others. You never know who God can help heal through you.

Lisa Johnson
President of Lisa Johnson HR Consulting

His Dialogue

*The Spirit God gave us does not make us timid,
but gives us power, love and self-discipline.*

2 Timothy 1:7

*F*ive years ago, I found myself in a season of change and felt the need to move forward. However, I had to face the fear of the unknown and address my insecurity about needing to be good enough. I believed my talent was not transferable to the new venture.

Then I remembered the above verse. The Lord taught me to boldly pursue new opportunities. He gave me clarity to make the right decision and provided me with love and support. I used His dialogue, instead of my own inner dialogue, to garner power and strength to face this new season. I am in awe of how He continues to bestow His blessings to ultimately shift my inner dialogue to His message of strength in the face of new challenges. Ask Him to give you clarity today and see where His strength takes you.

Tonia Degner
Sr. Leader at Amazon

Purposeful Is Not Importance

Many are the plans in a person's heart,
but it is the Lord's purpose that prevails.

Proverbs 19:21

Many confuse "purposeful" with "important." We should view "living purposefully" as understanding and acknowledging God's purpose for us. To overcomplicate the idea of living a purposeful life puts us in danger of never discovering that purpose.

How can you determine your purpose? Actively go to God, with an open heart and mind, with the intention of discovering His purpose for you, Once you know which direction you should be headed: go. As long as you're moving forward, and you know what you're accomplishing coincides with God's purpose for you, never lose hope.

Whether you're searching, have just begun, or have been following God's plan for years, let God guide you. Your life will be gratifying and have an eternal impact on others.

Diane Paddison
Founder of 4word women
Former Executive Team at Trammell Crow Company,
CBRE, and ProLogis

Walk on Water

Then Peter got down out of the boat,
walked on the water and came toward Jesus.

Matthew 14:29

*J*ust when you feel like you've seen it all, something hits you unexpectedly and you feel like your world is crashing down around you.

I'm reminded of Peter doing the impossible: walking on water. But Peter quickly becomes fearful of the wind and the waves and begins to sink. He cries out, and Jesus is there to save him.

How many times has this happened in your life? You want to trust God, but all your human brain can process are the circumstances. All you see are the waves, not the God who can walk on them.

Remember, tribulations make us resilient. In our tribulations we're reminded of God's continued faithfulness to us. Even in our doubting and fear, God reaches down and pulls us back to Him, so that we can say, like the disciples in the boat, "Truly you are the Son of God."

Sandra Crawford Williamson
CEO of Crawford Creative Consulting
4word Advisory Board Member

REFLECT & REFRESH

Have you ever had to take responsibility for a mistake or failure? How did doing so glorify God?

Are you searching for God's purpose? Ask Him to reveal His purpose to you—and then go!

How could sharing your story help others? Pray for both the courage and the opportunity to share your story boldly.

Lord, thank you for giving me a story. You have been with me through every season. Thank you for the struggles, hurts, and trials that have made me strong and resilient. When I make a mistake, help me be courageous and take responsibility in a way that glorifies you, regardless of the consequences. I know you don't waste a hurt, so give me boldness to share my story with others who need healing. Thank you for using all things for good.

Week 47

No Fairy Godmother

Blessed is the one who trusts in the Lord, who does not look to the proud, to those who turn aside to false gods.

Psalm 40:4

Sometimes, the best mentors may seem nothing like you, but they can speak powerfully into your life in ways you might never expect. This happened to a woman in the 4word Mentor Program. She was paired with a mentor who, at first glance, just didn't make sense for her. She wasn't pleased and "raved" at God in prayer. However, she felt strongly that God had called her to be part of the program and submitted to His plans for her. In the end, God used that unlikely match to bring deep things to her attention, with ramifications far beyond her career.

Trust that God has brought you and your mentor together for a reason. Dive into the process. Be vulnerable. Your mentor is no fairy godmother, but honestly, magic can happen.

Diane Paddison
Founder of 4word women
Former Executive Team at Trammell Crow Company, CBRE, and ProLogis

Wait and Listen

The heart of the discerning acquires knowledge,
for the ears of the wise seek it out.

Proverbs 18:15

*Y*ears ago, I needed a trustworthy woman outside of my current circle to help me navigate an extremely painful life experience. I made a list of what I needed from her. Then I asked God to lead me to the wise person who could counsel, and pray with me, about this issue.

Three weeks later, I was sitting across from a woman who stockpiled resources like no one I'd ever met. With open hands, she offered what she'd received along the way. How did I find her? *By waiting and listening.*

In our culture, we tend to rush impatiently, even through our hurts and our needs. The more we can use our tenacity to find the mentor we identify with best, the more satisfying life becomes. She's out there! Don't give up. Be persistent. Ask God to make her evident and to place His hand over your future connection.

Pamela Lau
Author, Teacher, and Speaker

Transitions

In the multitude of counselors there is safety.

Proverbs 11:14 NKJV

Transitions are hard. I'm normally a confident person, but after having served in the military for eleven years, I was uncertain about my future. The woman who became my future boss seemed to understand this fear. During my interview she told me, "I can sense you aren't sure about this career. Just come here, do a good job, and meet great people. Use this opportunity as your 'transition' job to figure out what you really want to do."

I'm so blessed that this woman (who became a mentor and friend) was direct, understanding, and gave me the freedom to figure out my professional and personal priorities. Her grace and understanding provided an amazing leadership example and a godly influence in a secular work environment. Whether they knew it or not, everyone who came in contact with her encountered Jesus. What better example of marrying spiritual and professional mentorship could there be?

Natasha Sistrunk Robinson
Author of *Mentor for Life: Finding Purpose through Intentional Discipleship*

Step Out and Seek

Open my eyes that I may see
wonderful things in your law.

Psalm 119:18

$\mathscr{E}$veryone needs a personal advisory board comprised of a coach to help you create and implement your strategic plan, mentors to share their experiences, and friends who will be brutally honest. Having women of faith on that team is a huge bonus. As we struggle to balance faith, family, and career, it's comforting and motivating to have a like-minded mentor as your accountability partner, cheerleader, and taskmaster.

If you need guidance, don't be afraid to ask for help! If there's someone you admire, tell her you'd love to learn how she got to where she is today. Women are genuinely interested in helping one another succeed, and most of us would be honored that someone wanted to learn from us.

Step out in faith and seek your mentor today. God just might have placed her in plain sight! You just have to be bold and ask.

Susan Tolles
4word Regional Director of Local Groups, Central

Mentor Misunderstandings

*In everything set them an example by doing what
is good. In your teaching show integrity, seriousness.*

Titus 2:7

I'm surprised by the number of young women who don't have mentors or who don't find them helpful. I think that comes from misunderstanding what mentors are—and are not.

The most important role of a mentor is to listen, ask questions, and provide thoughtful alternatives for you to consider. Mentors are advisors, generous with their time and efforts, and deserving of your appreciation and respect.

One of the things I love most about mentoring is seeing God work in someone's life (and mine) in totally unexpected ways. God laid out a model for mentoring in the Bible (in Titus 2 and elsewhere) to help believers grow. If you're struggling to find a mentor, or worrying that you have the "wrong" one, I encourage you to take a step in faith: trust God to work in that process for you.

Diane Paddison
Founder of 4word women
Former Executive Team at Trammell Crow Company,
CBRE, and ProLogis

REFLECT & REFRESH

Do you need a mentor? Make a list of the things you need from the counsel of a mentor, and ask God to provide the perfect woman to support you in this season.

How do you view the mentors in your life? Take the opportunity to express your gratitude to them this week.

Do you have a personal advisory board? Pray about who in your circle could offer wise counsel then boldly ask them to join your "board."

Lord, thank you for providing wise counsel through the mentors in my life. Help me be open to the wisdom and guidance of the women you have placed in my path, especially those that love and follow you. Give me an open mind and a heart willing to learn and grow, even from mentors who, on the surface, don't seem to quite "fit." Remind me to show gratitude to those who offer their time, energy, and support, and bring younger women into my life whom I can in turn offer a helping hand.

Week 48

Here to Glorify

Remember the Lord your God, for it is he who
gives you the ability to produce wealth.

Deuteronomy 8:18

We all should have disaster preparedness plans, but do you have a "spiritual preparedness plan"? Ask yourself, "If my life ended today, what would happen to me?" Then, "While I'm here on earth, what am I called to do?"

Ultimately, I'm here to glorify God. Living through Hurricane Sandy prompted me to revisit how I spend my time and money. The discomforts of the storm made me realize my powerlessness and reliance on the Lord and others.

Deuteronomy 8:18 shatters any illusions I have about taking care of myself and being self-sufficient. It is only because of God's hand that I have a job, the education to carry out my job, and the opportunities He's afforded me personally and professionally. My security is only found in the cross—not in my plans.

Marcia Peiffer
Former Manager of HR at *The Wall Street Journal*
Soccer Mom to 4

Open to Change

"The Lord your God is going with you!
He will fight for you against your enemies,
and he will give you victory!"

Deuteronomy 20:4 NLT

*W*hen my husband and I moved, we anticipated a year of "us" time, just enjoying being a couple and exploring the city. But while we were unpacking, we had a couple of crisis situations erupt in our family. Teilhard de Chardin's words, "Trust in the slow work of God," became my mantra.

Changing your location and style of living doesn't mean instant release from problems and crises–those follow you wherever you go. When you think you're about to embark on one thing and God throws a wrench in your plans, understand that your "detour" isn't a detour to Him. It's the direction you were originally supposed to be going. Be open to change with the confidence that God won't put you through something you can't handle!

Susy Flory
New York Times Best-selling Author and Coauthor

Spending Time

"Whatever you do, whether in word or deed,
do it all in the name of the Lord Jesus, giving thanks
to God the Father through him."

Colossians 3:17

*L*ooking back, I'm so thankful I put everything I could into using the gifts God's given me throughout my career. You never know when a season will hit where you don't have the opportunity to pour all of your energy into your work, because family matters or health issues have to take priority.

How can we know if God is pleased with the way we're spending our time in the season we are in? Consistent prayer. I pray about how I spend each day, week, and year. I trust God is leading me and will redirect me if I get off track.

God asks us to do the best we can with what He's entrusted to us. By doing this, we can ensure God is pleased with how we've spent our time.

Diane Paddison
Founder of 4word women
Former Executive Team at Trammell Crow Company,
CBRE, and ProLogis

Not Fair

*Whatever you do, work at it with all your heart,
as working for the Lord, not for human masters.*

Colossians 3:23

As children, we learn to expect fairness as we learn to follow the rules. We learn that rules exist to keep us safe and provide justice. When they're broken, someone inevitably proclaims, "That's not fair!"

We all encounter scenarios like these in the working world: the puzzling evaluation of underperformance, the teammate taking credit for your work, the time you're blamed for the failure of an entire project. Suddenly you're the one proclaiming, "That's not fair!"

When the fairness question arises, refocus on the lesson of Colossians 3:23. Who are you really working to please? Are you working to merely outperform a coworker? Is your motive only to avoid a bad review?

The workplace is not always a fair place. But that plays a minor role when we focus our heart on loving God and one another ... all the workday long.

Lisa Herbstreit
Finance Chair, 4word: Austin

What God Wants Done

God is our refuge and strength,
always ready to help in times of trouble.

Psalm 46:1 NLT

We often take on the world (e.g., career, family, church duties, simple chores) as if we're on a journey alone. So when things fail or go a different way, we cry out to God for help. Perhaps, the change in plans was a change to "our plans," not His.

We should present everything to God first, preparing our hearts for what He has in store. When the course changes or storms arise, we can simply adjust and keep going, comforted by knowing "He's got this." When we fully surrender our plans to Him, it's amazing to see how our careers change. Our desires change. Our ways change. Our faith changes. Our faith grows. We truly learn what it means to "trust in the Lord."

Our to-do list will be much more satisfying when it's filled with what *God* wants done.

Kathy F. Belton
Execution Planning Manager with ExxonMobil
Research & Engineering Company

List five things you are thankful for each day this week as a reminder that God is your ultimate provider.

Do you believe God is pleased with how you spend your time? If not, reflect on how you could manage your time differently.

Have you recently been treated unfairly at work? Meditate on Colossians 3:23, thinking about who you are really working to please.

Lord, I want to please you in the way I spend my time. Show me how I can reorganize my days and weeks to reflect your desires for my life, both at work and at home. I want to be able to confidently answer the question of what I am called to do on this earth and spend my time accordingly, never relying on my own power to accomplish that which you have called me to do. I surrender to you and your plans for my day, week, year, and life. May my to-do list only be filled with things that honor you.

Week 49

Blessings of All Sizes

So do not fear, for I am with you; do not be dismayed,
for I am your God. I will strengthen you and help you.

Isaiah 41:10

I've seen God's blessings exhibited in so many ways through my daughter Annie's health journey. Adam, Annie's boyfriend, came to our house one day with a friend and has been part of our lives ever since. Captain O'Grady, who flew the airplane that brought Annie home from surgery in California, cared for her like a loving member of a family.

Answers to our prayers for healing for Annie has been an amazing blessing. Even Annie's health condition is an unexpected blessing in another, profound way—it caused our family to focus on the "right things."

Blessings come in many shapes and sizes. What circumstance in your life seemed impossible but ended up bringing you incredible blessings? Praise Him in every season of life, for His way is perfect.

Diane Paddison
Founder of 4word women
Former Executive Team at Trammell Crow Company,
CBRE, and ProLogis

God's Detour

Commit your way to the Lord;
trust in him, and he will act.

Psalm 37:5 ESV

I costarred on TV's "Matlock" as Andy Griffith's law partner, Michelle. When I left the show, new project offers conflicted with my convictions, so I kept turning them down. Then the phone stopped ringing.

Months passed before a role was offered: host of a fashion and lifestyle series. *Host? No way! I'm an ACTOR!* But the phone still wasn't ringing. Unexcited, I took the job, with no idea of the path God had planned.

I wrote a blog for the show's website that led to my first book. Today I'm still acting *and* writing books and speaking to women around the world. Who could imagine that saying no and standing for my beliefs would ultimately reveal new gifts and deep fulfillment?

Nancy Stafford
Actress, Speaker, and Author of *The Wonder of His Love: A Journey into the Heart of God*

Unload Your Backpack

He leads me beside still waters.
He restores my soul.
Psalm 23:2–3 ESV

God had an amazing journey planned for you, traveling to the site of your God-given potential. You began with what you needed in your backpack, including unique gifts, passions, and personality traits for navigating life.

You encountered some big rocks along the way. Instead of tossing them over the edge of the path, you put them in your backpack. The longer you travel, the more rocks you collect. Eventually the burden is so heavy you cannot go on.

These rocks are the burdens of fear, perfectionism, doubt, and unhealthy relationships that you've been unable, or unwilling, to discard. If you'd let them go instead of dragging them along, you'd be so much closer to that beautiful place God intended for you to go.

Today, give those rocks to God. He's waiting to help you throw away the excess weight. In Him, find rest for your soul.

Susan Tolles
4word Regional Director of Local Groups, Central

What Do You Rely On?

Blessed is the one who trusts in the Lord,
whose confidence is in him.

Jeremiah 17:7

As a scrappy kid growing up in Detroit's inner city, I stood up to bullies, holding my own on the playground. I never dreamed I'd be running my own restaurant business. Yet here I was, CEO.

One night, all my joy and pride were shaken by a midnight call from the sheriff. My business had been bombed. But when God gives you a dream not even dynamite can make you run. I picked up the pieces and let God put them back together again. I realized people were watching my faith in the midst of adversity. Could I still serve God joyfully? I could, because of His promises.

Are you trusting the Lord or more focused on what you're accomplishing in your own strength? Keep your reliance on the One who's blessed you with everything you call "yours."

Kathryn M. Tack
Executive Coach of Executive Coach, Inc.
Former CEO of Good Times, a multimillion dollar franchise in hospitality/management
4word Board Member

Secular Seduction

*The path of the righteous is like the morning sun,
shining ever brighter till the full light of day.*

Proverbs 4:18

I believe we all face a "crisis moment" when we realize just how important it is to live out our faith in the midst of challenging secular environments. While I'm blessed to now oversee a team of amazing women who put Jesus first, there were many seasons when I had to learn to navigate workplace environments that challenged who I was and what I believed.

Our identity as Christians can be tested in the workplace in many ways. If women aren't in the marketplace, where most people spend the majority of their waking hours, we don't have the opportunity to meet people "where they are" and show them what it looks like to put Jesus first.

Be a valuable member of your workplace without falling victim to the secular seduction that can snake its way into office culture.

Diane Paddison
Founder of 4word women
Former Executive Team at Trammell Crow Company,
CBRE, and ProLogis

REFLECT & REFRESH

Are you focused on the "right things"? How have difficult circumstances helped you reset your priorities?

What rocks are you carrying that are weighing you down? Ask God to reveal any burdens you are carrying that He wants you to give to Him.

Have you fallen victim to "secular seduction" in your workplace? What can you do this week to show your coworkers what it looks like to put Jesus first?

Lord, I want to be focused on the right things— things that are true, noble, right, pure, lovely, and admirable. Use the circumstances of my life, even the most difficult ones, to refine me and draw me closer to you. I lay down every rock I have picked up along the journey of my life, knowing that your desire is for me to walk in freedom. Help me to trust and rely on you instead of trying to accomplish things in my own strength, so that others can see what a life dedicated to following you looks like.

Week 50

Never Sacrifice Home

Marriage should be honored by all.

Hebrews 13:4

I wouldn't be where I am today without my husband. He's been my prayer warrior, my constant support, a comedian when I needed to lighten up, and my helpmate in every way.

Yet I had to learn to allow him to do this. I had to learn to let go of laundry, loading the dishwasher my way, dressing our daughter every morning, etc. We do things differently, but different isn't bad; it's just different. I could run myself into the ground trying to do everything or make this a team effort.

Never sacrifice home in the name of work. I'm convinced God did not call us to sacrifice our marriage or family in the name of ministry or climbing the career ladder. Establish boundaries and be diligent in asking God to help reinforce them. Cherish the relationships He's placed in your life. Your time and dedication to them will far outweigh any professional glory.

Julie Baumgardner
President and CEO of First Things First

Lost in the Rush

For we are His workmanship,
created in Christ Jesus for good works.

Ephesians 2:10 NASB

"Workmanship" in the original Greek is *poiéma,* which gives us our English words poem and poetry. You are God's poem, His masterpiece, His divine work of art.

We easily lose sight of this in the rush of everyday life. How can I feel like a masterpiece when I'm just trying to feed my family and do my job? Start by choosing to believe God. He speaks truth. He's been planning you and your good works long before you showed up on the planet.

Then ask God what good works does He have for you today? What good works does He want you to be moving toward? Resolve to listen for the answers. Keep asking and write down what you hear. Then obey, even if it seems that answer doesn't make sense.

God will gradually reveal those good works. Ask. Listen. Obey. Repeat. Today and every day.

Wende Gaikema
Career and Life Coach

Satisfied

Praise the Lord, my soul, and forget not all his benefits
... who redeems your life from the pit and crowns
you with love and compassion, who satisfies
your desires with good things.

Psalm 103:2, 4–5

*I*n our busyness, our relationship with our spouse can easily slip to the back burner. We start feeling lonely in the chaos. We're in a vulnerable place and don't even realize it.

That's when we get the friend request from the sweet guy that has no idea what our life looks like now. He likes a photo of our kids on social media, commenting, "You're an awesome mom." He follows us on Instagram and compliments our creativity. His validation grips our attention-starved heart.

If you find yourself staring at a friend request like this, *delete it*. If you're already innocently chatting with someone, *stop*. Find a friend or counselor you trust and share your thoughts.

The truth is that the validation of our heart *will never be satisfied* outside of Christ.

Sandra Crawford Williamson
CEO of Crawford Creative Consulting
4word Advisory Board Member

Greater Mission

The one who has knowledge uses words with restraint,
and whoever has understanding is even-tempered.

Proverbs 17:27

The typical office annoyance usually starts with something small, but can quickly escalate. If something is bothering you at work, there are two options for handling it in a healthy way: try to work it out with the person responsible or choose to let it go.

That guy clicking his pen in the meeting next to you? He's annoying, sure, but he's God's creation. You're called to love him as Christ loved us.

Sometimes you really do need to confront someone about something they're doing, especially if it's having a significant impact on your work. Try to approach those situations with grace and respect. Look for positive changes that could resolve the situation.

Whatever may be bothering you about your workplace, remember that the purpose of your work is not your own comfort. It's to serve God and His greater mission.

Diane Paddison
Founder of 4word women
Former Executive Team at Trammell Crow Company,
CBRE, and ProLogis

Invite the Lord

You will keep in perfect peace those whose
minds are steadfast, because they trust in you.

Isaiah 26:3

My dad was a pastor. Growing up, this provided me
with a front row seat to one of the best leadership
courses available. There always seemed to be a crisis or
something to resolve—people issues, staffing challenges,
financial hurdles, etc.

However, there also seemed to be a sense of calm and
peace through it all. As I got older, I was able to understand and appreciate the approach my dad had taken. He
often whispered a prayer or "disappeared" to a quiet place.
In those times, he was inviting the Lord into the process.
Without fail, everything seemed to work out as planned or,
in many cases, even better.

As leaders, we have to take the same approach: invite
the Lord into the process, no matter how big or small.
When our plans are committed to Him first, things have a
way of working out.

Kathy F. Belton
Execution Planning Manager with ExxonMobil
Research & Engineering Company

REFLECT & REFRESH

Have you ever sacrificed home and family for the sake of work? Ask God to help you establish and reinforce boundaries between work and home.

Set aside fifteen minutes for prayer today. Ask God what good works He has for you, and write down what you hear Him say.

What safeguards can you put in place to protect you from temptations and unhealthy relationships at work?

Lord, thank you that I am your workmanship— your perfect masterpiece. I choose to believe that you created me with a purpose and want what is best for me. When I fall into the trap of putting work ahead of my family, show me how to set firm boundaries and put my relationships first. Guard my heart from temptation and help me pursue relationships that honor and point others to you. I commit to seeking your desires for my life, setting aside the time to truly wait and listen. Reveal yourself to me as I seek you.

Week 51

Shining Example

Start children off on the way they should go,
and even when they are old they will not turn from it.

Proverbs 22:6

I've been reflecting on how my feelings about my mom have changed through my lifetime—and how what my kids think of me will change too.

Recently, I tried karaoke at a birthday party. Who doesn't want to hear their mom sing Bon Jovi? Apparently, my daughter. I suddenly morphed from her standard of beauty, coolness, and womanhood to a source of embarrassment. Yikes!

I love and adore my children, wanting every good thing for them. I now realize that's how much my mother loves me. I can't go back and change my adolescent attitude toward my mom. But what I can do is obediently honor my mom now. As my children watch me lovingly respect my parents, they will see a shining example of how God wants them to treat me.

Sandra Crawford Williamson
CEO of Crawford Creative Consulting
4word Advisory Board Member

Serenity

The Lord gives strength to his people;
the Lord blesses his people with peace.

Psalm 29:11

*P*eace and relationships—sometimes, it seems like we can have either or, but not both. The root of the problem may lie outside of ourselves, but sometimes we have to look inward.

One common relational coping strategy is control. In an effort to make things seem peaceful or stable, we try to control others' actions or feelings. While that may feel satisfying in the short term, it can create wounds, stemming from bitterness, rebellion, and anger in those around us.

Instead, try using the Serenity Prayer to help you choose what to get involved in: "God, grant me the serenity to accept the things I cannot change; the courage to change the things I can; and the wisdom to know the difference."*

Ask yourself: "Can I change this person's beliefs, thoughts, or behaviors?" If the answer is no, then choose to make a difference in your response and in what you can control.

Wende Gaikema
Career and Life Coach

---

* Reinhold Niebuhr, "The Serenity Prayer," *Crypton* (June 7, 2017).

Core Identity

As a father has compassion on his children,
so the Lord has compassion on those who fear him.

Psalm 103:13

There's mounting evidence to support that a girl's core beliefs and future identity as a woman is directly shaped by her connection (or lack thereof) with her dad.

How we interface with our father sets the foundation for how we come to understand God as a Father. If the relationship with your earthly father has been secure, consistent, fair, loving, and safe, you'll most often project those qualities onto Father God. When the opposite is true, God may be the last person a wounded woman wants to trust.

The great news is that our Abba Father God loves us with a forever love. There's nothing we can do (or not do) to change that fact! The more we come to know our real Dad and internalize His view of us, the more vibrant and secure we'll be in our true identity.

Michelle Watson, PhD, LPC

Sense of Timing

We also thank God continually because,
when you received the word of God, which you heard
from us, you accepted it not as a human word,
but as it actually is, the word of God.

1 Thessalonians 2:13

*I*f you're at a crossroads with your career, there are a few steps you can take to help determine what comes next. First, get on the same page as God. I'm finally at the place where I can pray, "Lord, whatever you want me to do, I'm willing."

Next, adjust your sense of timing. I wanted to quickly jump into a new career, but needed to learn a few things about myself and God first. If you're unsure what God is calling you to, get help from professionals who've already traveled this road.

Finally, cling to God, even when you can't understand what He's doing. The longer and more difficult the process becomes, the more time you should spend at His feet.

Rhonda S. Kehlbeck PhD
Director of Admissions of The Halftime Institute

Value the Opportunity

I cry out to God Most High,
to God who fulfills his purpose for me.

Psalm 57:2 ESV

I don't mind admitting I'm glad I raised my children before the age of Pinterest, Facebook, Instagram, and the like. All those communication tools can be useful and fun, but they're also full of something that can be any woman's undoing: "the more."

"The more" represents everything you're not doing. It's all the networking events you don't make it to, the fundraisers you decline, the adorable animal-shaped sandwiches you're not making for your children, the "top ten" Bible verses you haven't memorized yet.

Pay close attention to what your gifts and priorities are. Value the opportunity to slow down and focus on doing a few things well. Doing less is less exciting, but it's also more fulfilling. A fulfilling life is what God wants for all of His children, and with His guidance, you will find one.

Diane Paddison
Founder of 4word women
Former Executive Team at Trammell Crow Company,
CBRE, and ProLogis

REFLECT & REFRESH

Are you tempted to control others? Instead of trying to change a coworker or family member, choose to make a difference in your own response to the situation.

In what areas of your life are you tempted by the "more"?

Has your relationship with your own parents shaped how you view God? Ask God to show you who He is as your Abba Father.

Lord, thank you that as your daughter, I am enough. Keep any troubled relationships I've had in my past from skewing my view of you. I know that I don't have to chase after "more" in order to be fulfilled, because I have everything I need in you. Give me wisdom to know what I should pursue and what is not part of your plan for my life. Help me stand against the temptations of our culture to do more, have more, and be more. I want to rest in you, knowing that I am the daughter of Abba Father, and nothing can ever change that.

Week 52

Stop Apologizing

For the Lord will be your confidence.

Proverbs 3:26 NKJV

*B*eing a great leader is a way of life and is not dependent on a job title. We are all made for a greater purpose in this life, and focusing on the bigger picture helps us become great leaders through our daily behaviors.

Female leaders need to be bold and stop apologizing so much (myself included). Jack Welch taught me that, "Giving people self-confidence is by far the most important thing that I can do. Because then they will act." You have to be self-confident to give self-confidence to someone else. Know who you are in Christ and seek out a mentor to help you along the way.

Every single day is an opportunity to show the love of God to someone you meet. The business world is a mission field waiting for all of us to pour love into and change lives for the kingdom of God.

Meg Weinkauf
Founder of The Faithful Leader

Restoration

> "I will restore the fortunes of Jacob's tents and have compassion on his dwellings; the city will be rebuilt on her ruins, and the palace will stand in its proper place."
>
> *Jeremiah 30:18*

My favorite part of working as a designer at Magnolia Homes is the restoration work. We take old, worn, broken things, and put life and beauty back into them. God does this very thing in our lives and hearts.

We've had clients with broken pasts. We have the chance to give families a safe place to restart, an oasis of peace and hope. We pray that God is using our team to touch families all over for His glory, and that His kingdom will stand in the rightful place in our lives.

Ask God today to open your eyes to see the broken people around you who have wonderful potential. Sow into seeing them redeemed and restored through prayer, encouragement, and love. God wants you to be the hands and feet of this renovation.

Laura Stafford
Designer for Joanna Gaines at Magnolia

Walk Humbly

"Remember the Lord, who is great and awesome,
and fight for your families, your sons and
your daughters, your wives and your homes."

Nehemiah 4:14

*I*n 1997, our family embarked on our first mission trip through a foundation we established. Nothing bonds you quite like roughing it in Africa together. As our kids grew, we realized we could do more as a family than as individuals, utilizing their law degrees and professional experiences as a platform for outreach and ministry.

Working together helps us appreciate the unique gifts and talents God has bestowed on each of us. On our mission projects, we spend time together in prayer and devotions each day. It's a way to keep our eyes off ourselves and our discomfort and to maintain family harmony.

As a family, service is a way of life. It's what God's called us to, the theme of The Micah Global Foundation: "to do justly, and to love mercy, and to walk humbly" (Micah 6:8 KJV).

Margaret Larson
Executive Director of Micah Global Foundation

Faith's Impact

Jesus answered, "I am the way and
the truth and the life. No one comes to
the Father except through me."

John 14:6

*O*ne of my favorite Christian missionaries told me, "Speak in Bible verses, never quote chapter and verse." Biblical teaching is central to my approach to work and life. I attempt to evidence these teachings in everyday situations, without quoting chapter and verse. I believe it's better for people to experience the love and teaching of Jesus, than to hear it preached by your boss.

If you know your team well and spend a lot of time with them, you will have many opportunities to mention how faith impacts your life—and opportunities for people to ask you about your faith. I look for these natural moments in a trusted relationship, and offer words of encouragement to those seeking deeper knowledge or deeper faith.

Cheryl Bachelder
Former CEO of Popeyes Louisiana Kitchen, Inc.
Named the world's top CEO by *Inc.* magazine (June 8, 2017)
Author of *Dare to Serve: How to Drive Superior Results by Serving Others*

Find Your Community

Accept one another, then, just as Christ accepted you,
in order to bring praise to God.

Romans 15:7

*P*eople aren't meant to be solitary creatures. God created in us a need to know and to be known. He uses people in our lives to minister to our bodies and souls, to build humility in our hearts, and speak truth to our ears.

When life feels heavy, it's easy to fall into isolation. Many breadwinners have trouble connecting with other Christian women like them. It's not that we can only be friends with women whose lives look like ours, but it sure helps to have a few good friends who've faced similar challenges.

If you have these women in your life, cling to them. If you don't, it's time to start looking! Pray that God would bring some women into your life. Then be ready to step out in faith when He does.

Diane Paddison
Founder of 4word women
Former Executive Team at Trammell Crow Company,
CBRE, and ProLogis

REFLECT & REFRESH

Do you find yourself over-apologizing? What's one step you can take this week to become more self-confident at work?

Ask God to open your eyes to see the broken people around you. Commit to showing them love and encouragement in a tangible way this week.

Seek an opportunity to share how your faith impacts your life with your coworkers this week.

> Lord, thank you for the opportunities you give me each day to live out my faith at work, at home, and in my community. I'm blessed to be your hands and feet to the world around me. Teach me to live with bold faith. Give me eyes to see the brokenness around me, so I can extend your love to those who need it. Above all, I want to know you and your plan for my life. Reveal to me the path forward, and I will walk in it.

About the Authors

Diane Paddison, 4word women Founder and President, is a Harvard MBA graduate, former global executive of two Fortune 500 companies and one Fortune 1000 company, and serves as an independent director for two corporations and four organizations, one being the Salvation Army's National Advisory Board. A leading advocate for Christian women in the workplace, Diane published *Work, Love, Pray* in 2011, laying the foundation for 4word women. She authors weekly posts at 4wordwomen.org and is a featured columnist for other publications. Diane and her husband, Chris, have four children and live in Dallas, Texas.

Jordan Johnstone, 4word Digital Community Manager, is a working mom in Atlanta, Georgia, who spends her days balancing her dream career as a writer and creative communicator, and her dream role as a mom and wife. Jordan holds an MFA in Creative Writing from Full Sail University and a BS in Advertising and Public Relations from Liberty

University. She writes weekly on 4wordwomen.org and oversees the digital community team as they work to reach the global community of women in the workplace.

•••

This devotional features the words and wisdom of more than a hundred professionals from all industries and leadership levels, seeking to encourage and embolden the life of every woman in the workplace who picks up this book. The "Reflect & Refresh" pages were authored by Caitie Butler, the 4word Church Connect Program Manager.

4word

get involved

Start cultivating a global community of real, passionate, faithful women who are boldly living out Christ's calling on their lives, just as you do everyday.

find us online

Online at 4wordwomen.org is the fastest way to learn more. Weekly blog posts and interviews, videos, resources are all free and we even have a membership where you get even more access.

join a local group

Local groups connect and strengthen the community of professional Christian women at different gatherings and luncheons with speakers, studies, and social events.

engage in a mentorship

This program facilitates a relationship between two women who share accountability to help a mentee work toward her professional, personal and spiritual goals.

4wordwomen.org

Notes

Notes

Notes

Notes

4wordwomen.org